P9-EGB-300

THE TRIUMPHANT SPIRIT

THE TRIUMPHANT SPIRIT

PORTRAITS & STORIES OF HOLOCAUST SURVIVORS ...
THEIR MESSAGES OF HOPE & COMPASSION

CREATED & PHOTOGRAPHED BY

NICK DEL CALZO

STORIES WRITTEN BY RENEE ROCKFORD

INTERVIEWS BY NICK DEL CALZO

STORY TEXT CONTRIBUTED BY DREW MYRON & NICK DEL CALZO

EDITED BY LINDA J. RAPER

INTRODUCTION BY THOMAS KENEALLY
AUTHOR OF *SCHINDLER'S LIST*

FOREWORD BY JAN KARSKI, PH.D.
FORMER POLISH DIPLOMAT & HONORED RESCUER

Published by

TRIUMPHANT SPIRIT™ PUBLISHING

P.O. Box 19129

Denver, CO 80219

(303) 986-1919; Fax: (303) 986-0123

This book, or any portions thereof, may not be reproduced
in any form without written permission of the publisher.

Copyright © 1997 by Nick Del Calzo.

All rights reserved.

Designed by Carrie Ammon Jordan

Production prints by Bernard R. Lange,

  Pallas PhotoImaging, Inc. of Denver, CO

Duotones by Digital World Images

Printed in Seoul, Korea by Sung In Printing America, Inc.

ISBN 0-9655260-0-3 (hardbound)

ISBN 0-9655260-1-1 (softbound)

COVER: portrait of Emil Gold and Zesa Starr

PAGE 1: portrait of Moritz Goldfeier

PAGE 2: portrait of Jacob Meller

ACQUISITION OF PRINTS

Museum-quality prints of the portraits in this book and in the project archives are available for purchase through THE TRIUMPHANT SPIRIT FOUNDATION. Interested institutions, corporate collectors, and private individuals can obtain further information about prices and availability by contacting:

THE TRIUMPHANT SPIRIT FOUNDATION

P.O. Box 19129

Denver, Colorado 80219

(303) 986-1919   Fax: (303) 986-0123

PROCEEDS

A portion of the proceeds from the sale of this book will help support the mission of THE TRIUMPHANT SPIRIT FOUNDATION, a nonprofit organization dedicated to visual initiatives with an educational and humanitarian directive.

NATIONAL EXHIBITION

A traveling portrait exhibition of the images in this book is available through THE TRIUMPHANT SPIRIT FOUNDATION. Inquiries should be directed to the address listed below.

THE TRIUMPHANT SPIRIT FOUNDATION

P.O. Box 19129

Denver, Colorado 80219

(303) 986-1919   Fax: (303) 986-0123

DEDICATION

To those six million

Holocaust souls

whose gifted spirit

never had a chance

to triumph.

CONTENTS

TRIUMPH OF THE SPIRIT

INTRODUCTION BY THOMAS KENEALLY, AUTHOR OF SCHINDLER'S LIST

The first Holocaust survivors I ever spoke to at any meaningful length were Leopold Pfefferberg Page and his wife, Ludmila. Leopold is featured in *The Triumphant Spirit* along with a number of other brave souls.

Leopold came from prewar Krakow, that most civilized of cities, and Ludmila was a child of physicians from Lodz, Poland. They are veterans of the Krakow ghetto, of the Plaszow camp, in Mila's case of Auschwitz, and then of Schindler's labor camp at Brünnlitz in Moravia. When I first met them in 1980 they were running a small business in Beverly Hills. The more I got to know them, and the more I met other survivors, the more I began to perceive that, on a daily, if not hourly basis, all survivors needed somehow to negotiate their histories.

Daily and nightly, they are forced to face the claims their memories of unspeakable savagery make on them. Each day the phantoms, the terror of sneering, mechanical death, and even the guilt of survival, threaten to turn all their hearts to ashes and their sensibilities to stone.

There was a consistency between that first meeting with the Pages and all the subsequent meetings I was honored to have with other survivors. Survivors are often small or average-sized, compact people, but they burn with a towering ardor. I met apparently ordinary people in apparently ordinary living rooms of varying affluence, but from their lips nightmarish tales fell—tales of the collapse of a moral order, of the utter denial of the European and human fraternity.

After a time it was not so much their survival then, between 1939 and 1945, that amazed me—even though the odds against survival were so massive. It is the fact that the survival of horror did not in itself destroy them now. That is, the miracle seems that they are willing to have pictures on the wall, to sit on furniture made by other humans, and display family pictures on mantelpieces and pianos.

The miracle seems to be that they are willing to make these investments in the present structures of daily life, when their entire education under the Nazis and their collaborators has taught them that the human species, roused to its favorite passion of race hate, cannot be trusted. It is that, having survived, they have practiced the skills of living all over again. They have practiced them in DP (Displaced Persons) camps and in great American cities upon their disoriented arrival. They have practiced them in the midst of the long hours of their American labors, practiced them by risking their American children in the open, dangerous air. With the risk-taking, which is the better side of their unquenchable lives, they have remade themselves—more robustly than I know I ever could have done in similar circumstances. They invest themselves and their children in us, the untried masses of the new world, who have never been through the same things they had. They honor us with normal conversation and, on occasion, entrust to us glimpses of the cannibal era, of barbarities done to them in the name of race hysteria.

These men and women are consumed by a need to ensure that the rest of us believe in the authenticity of what they went through. They have been forced to this by an extraordinary phenomenon. The world accepts the validity of other hecatombs of this bloody century: No one denies the massacre of non-Jewish Poles by both Soviets and Nazis. No one denies the vengeance Stalin brought down on fellow Slavs, such as the Ukrainians. No one denies the slaughter of the Armenians. No one denies the killing fields of Cambodia. No one denies any of the other savageries of World War II, including Nagasaki and Hiroshima. And yet, the uniquely constructed and state-implemented process called the Holocaust is almost routinely questioned, denied, explained away, or minimized.

This, too, the people of *The Triumphant Spirit* must now struggle with—not only the horror they saw, but the denial of that horror. With this grief added to the grief of memory, look at the portraits in this book and tell me that their composure, their human grace, is not a triumph of spirit.

They have turned their faces to the camera of Nick Del Calzo who has lovingly photographed them. They are aware that their time on earth is not as extensive as it was when they were first rescued and brought to America. They want us, and others as yet unborn, to see in this book some of the evidence of what they were subjected to and what they have surmounted. I congratulate them on their survival and on appearing here, showing their human faces to us, and I congratulate Nick Del Calzo for having the initiative to bring this project to fruition.

FOREWORD

JAN KARSKI, PH.D., *PROFESSOR, RECIPIENT OF THE HONORARY CITIZENSHIP AWARD FROM THE STATE OF ISRAEL ON MAY 12, 1994 & DISTINGUISHED AND HONORED RESCUER*

May 12, 1994, became the most meaningful day in my life. On that day, the State of Israel made me an honorary citizen—and I reached the spiritual high of my Christian faith.

"I was born in Lodz, Poland, in 1914. In my high school, there were many Jewish students. They helped me in mathematics, physics, and chemistry. I helped them in Polish literature and history. We helped each other. Since those early years of my youth, I have been getting from the Jews: goodwill, friendship, and help.

"Our Lord revealed himself to many nations in His own way, but always with the same commandment: 'Love your neighbor.' Thus, religious tolerance and respect for each other became our sacred duty. We have an infinite capacity to do good and an infinite capacity to do evil. It is up to every one of us to make a choice. Our Lord endowed us with a free will. Let us then oppose and combat religious intolerance, fanaticism, anti-Semitism, and racism. They are sinful. They are also stupid. They stand in the way of progress.

"I have been teaching at Georgetown University—a Jesuit institution—for more than 40 years. In our school of Foreign Service, we have students of all religions, races, and nationalities.

Some of them consider it their duty not only to preserve, but also to propagandize their national, ethnic, or tribal traditions as being superior to others. It has been a wonderful experience for me to tell them, 'Preserve your national, ethnic, and cultural tradition, if you so wish. But also keep your minds open. There is much in our traditions that should be discarded—prejudices, false national myths, ethnic slurs, irrational rituals, and practices. The world is changing, advancing, and we must change, too. Cultural and religious pluralism, economic integration, interdependence of states and nations, and national pragmatism will mark our future.'

"I understand the uniqueness of the Holocaust. I saw it. We cannot let history forget it. The Jews were abandoned by governments, by church hierarchies, and by societal structures. But they were not abandoned by all humanity. Thousands upon thousands of individuals—priests and nuns, workers and peasants, educated ones, and simpletons—risked their lives or freedom to help the helpless Jews—in Poland, Holland, Belgium, France, Denmark, and Norway. Some of them have been publicly recognized, most of them remain unknown. We cannot let history forget them."

PREFACE

One highly acclaimed witness to mankind's most grotesque episode in recorded history said it best:

"People can live without pleasure but not without hope."

Holocaust survivor and celebrated author Nechama Tec summoned these poignant words from the depths of her soul after half a century of living with the memories of humanity's darkest hours.

Yet these nine words have a renewed, powerful meaning for the youth of our nation, many of whom have jettisoned any possibility of living a full, abundant life in pursuit of their dreams. Instead, they feel oppressed, disheartened, angry, and vengeful. Amid this emotional and spiritual fog, significant numbers of today's youth fail to grasp that they live in a free society, and that within America's borders reside vast educational resources and opportunities.

Out of the depths of mankind's darkness emerge inspiring messages from individuals who had every reason *not* to have hope. These extraordinary individuals are bright beacons for all humanity, and their stories rekindle the human spirit in each of us.

These portrayals present Holocaust witnesses who came to America, spiritually ignited by Miss Liberty's torch of freedom. Within days after reaching our shores, they became productive citizens. These *new* Americans established careers, built successful businesses, rebuilt their families, and made many positive contributions to the social and economic fabric of our community.

These inspiring examples also underscore important values that have begun to fade, but which need to be embraced again by all Americans, regardless of age, religious beliefs, or social and ethnic origin. These commemorative portraits and stories illuminate the American Dream. As it came true for them, so it can for the youth of our nation, too. Each person can truly fulfill his or her constitutional guarantee of "life, liberty, and the pursuit of happiness."

The Triumphant Spirit is more than a reminder about the Holocaust a half century ago. These images and stories transmit a unified theme of present-day hope, compassion, and tolerance.

Self-fulfillment is achievable for those who embrace a personal vision, possess an unswerving determination, take advantage of educational resources, and *never* abandon hope. These values form a rich palette of opportunities from which everyone may begin to create his or her own dreamscapes.

— *NICK DEL CALZO*

HARRY BASS & ELI OKON

BASS: RETIRED MARKET OWNER, COFOUNDER OF THE ASSOCIATION OF
JEWISH HOLOCAUST SURVIVORS & SURVIVOR OF AUSCHWITZ CONCENTRATION CAMP
OKON: RETIRED BAKER & SURVIVOR OF AUSCHWITZ AND DACHAU CONCENTRATION CAMPS

Elie Wiesel once said, "Survivors are understood by survivors alone. They speak in code. All outsiders could do, was to come close to the gates. Those who were not in Auschwitz will never enter Auschwitz."

Harry Bass and Eli Okon not only share the nightmares of Auschwitz, but also these childhood, lifelong friends share a story of survival.

"We went through terrible times," Okon says of his friend with whom he grew up. "There are nightmares still," he says, and when the two speak of the past, it is in code and, then, with a silence and emotion that render words useless. "There are things I will never forget in my entire life ... the crying, the screaming."

Bass and Okon were born in Bialystok, Poland. Bass was one of six children and Okon the youngest of eight. In 1939, their serene lives came to an abrupt end when the Russian Army occupied Poland. By 1941, the horror for the Jews in Bialystok began as German troops invaded their hometown, Okon says with his voice trailing. Okon vividly recalls when the Nazis marched into the city and set the synagogue on fire. There were 3,000 people inside and all died.

Bass was held in the Bialystok ghetto from 1941 to 1942 before being sent to the Pruzhany ghetto for one year. In 1943, he was sent to Auschwitz, where he remained until January 18, 1945. In the cold of January, he and thousands of other Jews were forced on a death march that lasted until mid-April.

Okon, meanwhile, lost his entire family at the hands of the Nazis and was sent from one labor camp to another, from Blizin to Sachsenhausen and from Auschwitz to Dachau. In 1945, he, too, was forced on a death march and escaped.

Soon after, the Americans liberated Dachau on April 29, and Okon was free. Bass was liberated just days later in Hamburg on May 3, 1945. He, too, had lost members of his family, his mother and three brothers.

Bass and Okon knew nothing of each other's whereabouts. They searched for each other, and, with the help of friends, were reunited in Munich. "We were so happy to see each other," recalls Okon. "We cried together, we were so happy."

They both immigrated to the United States. Harry Bass married, and he and his wife, Frances, raised a son. He found a job as a butcher before opening his own meat shop. He went on to own and operate numerous butcher shops and retired in 1981. Harry is a founder of the Association of Jewish Holocaust Survivors in Philadelphia, served as the organization's first president, and is currently vice president.

In 1946, Eli Okon married a Hungarian girl he had met in the labor camp. Their daughter was born in Germany. The family then moved to Israel in 1948 where their son was born. In 1960, they came to the United States. Their family has now grown to include five grandchildren. Today, he is a retired baker, the same profession of his parents decades earlier in Bialystok.

Just as they had been together in what Wiesel described as the "kingdom of night and nightmares," Bass and Okon remain close today, drawing strength from their memories. They live only minutes away from one another in Philadelphia.

> *"Our survival is a miracle. It's hard to understand what people will do to one another. We may forgive, but we may not so easily forget."*

13

MIRIAM BELL

COMMUNITY VOLUNTEER & SURVIVOR OF THE GHETTO AND BERGEN-BELSEN AND OTHER CONCENTRATION CAMPS

Miriam Bell was 10 years old when she and her family watched a Nazi execute her father on the streets of the ghetto. It was in 1941, just one day after they had left their home in Lithuania. "My mother covered my face and told me not to move, but I saw everything and heard the Nazis say that this will happen to every dirty Jew. I will never be able to erase that from my memory." Just a few weeks after her father's burial, her youngest sister and grandmother were also shot in the ghetto—part of a Nazi program to eliminate the very young and the very old.

Born in 1930 as Miriam Galperin, she was one of seven children. Her longtime family business specialized in transportation, buying and selling horses and wagons. Bell remembers they made a very comfortable living and had a very happy family life.

The slaughter of her family continued. Shortly after the most recent family killings, Bell and a brother and sister were transported in closed freight cars to a concentration camp in Estonia. Her mother and three other siblings were left behind in the ghetto. She discovered her sister had died when she recognized the little girl's clothes lying on a heap of prisoners' belongings at the camp. The girl had never made it alive to the camp, but suffocated while in transit in the overcrowded freight car.

Between 1942 and 1945, Miriam was moved to several other camps including Stutthof and Bergen Belsen. "With each stop at a different camp, there was mass hysteria and panic. Jews were fighting to survive … the freight cars were so crowded, many were dead on arrival." For more than a year, Bell worked in a Nazi ammunition factory—being beaten by guards as she worked. In one attack, several upper front teeth were broken. On another occasion, her nose was broken. She was never treated for any of her wounds, nor was she treated for two bouts of typhoid fever. "There were many other sick people in the same room and death beside me was a daily occurrence." She ate very little bread and water, and, by the end of the war, weighed just 79 pounds. Her liberation came in 1945.

Too sick to walk, Miriam was hospitalized. Later her search for her family found only news of their deaths. Her mother was killed in Stutthof, and a brother was killed in another camp. The others left behind in the ghetto were murdered by the SS. She had no news about the brother who had entered the camps with her in 1942. Then, 14 years after the war, she learned that he was being treated in a Russian sanitarium for tuberculosis.

After liberation, she was sent to an orphanage where she took nursing courses. She remembered people in her family who had studied medicine, including an aunt who was a pediatrician in Lithuania. She, too, perished in the camps.

By 1948, Miriam Bell had left Europe and settled in Canada, and later immigrated to the United States. Since then, she has dedicated her life to the nursing profession and worked in a hospital. She also volunteers for a variety of organizations including the Martyrs Memorial and Museum of the Holocaust in Los Angeles. "I tell my grandchildren, 'Be honest and proud of your Jewish heritage, and fight so that a Holocaust should never happen again.'"

> *"Everything we survivors contribute to humanity helps us to be human again. From the ashes we rose, with modesty we contribute."*

JUDY BERNEMAN & HELEN FIREMAN

RETIRED TAILORS & SURVIVORS OF AUSCHWITZ, HINDENBURG, AND BERGEN-BELSEN CONCENTRATION CAMPS

There were thousands of women and all of them were looking for a piece of grass to eat. That is how Judy Berneman remembers Bergen-Belsen where she and her sister, Helen Fireman, spent part of World War II.

Judy and Helen grew up in Pionki, Poland. Born Guta and Helen Weizman, the two sisters survived the Auschwitz, Hindenburg, and Bergen-Belsen concentration camps in 1944 and 1945.

Helen was engaged to be married to Sam Fireman, who owned a sheet metal company in Sosnowiec, some 300 miles away from her hometown. One night after the war started, Sam was ordered to report as a Jew to the Nazis. The next day Sam escaped with Helen from Sosnowiec to Pionki, and married her in 1940. They were imprisoned together in the ghetto and later taken to work in a munitions factory. In 1943, Helen, Judy, and Sam were deported to Auschwitz, where Sam was separated from his wife. Helen was reunited with her husband several weeks after liberation.

Judy met her husband, Abraham Berneman, during the war when they were assigned to work as tailors repairing gloves and uniforms for the Nazis. They worked together by day and returned to their separate barracks at night. All the while, the two sisters had each other.

"We would keep our will to live by clinging to the smallest hope. We were starving to death but we hoped it would get better." Judy recalls the many deaths she witnessed. "A good friend died in my lap, but that was not the worst of it. Every morning, we found 10 or 15 girls who had electrocuted themselves on the electrical barbed wires."

Throughout her ordeal, Judy managed to save a gold piece that her father had given her, along with a single bill of money. Both were hidden in her shoe. Had they been discovered, she would have been executed. In a desperate effort to save her cousin's life, Judy gave the bill to a woman, a camp guard who doled out soup in the camps, so that she could get an extra portion. Following the exchange, Judy went back for the extra portion. Instead of getting soup, the woman severely beat Judy.

The two sisters were liberated from Bergen-Belsen on April 21, 1945. Just weeks before liberation, their father was murdered in the camps. In 1949, they immigrated to America with their mother, Ryenka, and their two brothers, all of whom survived concentration camps. Judy came with her new husband, Abraham, and their baby daughter. Helen and Sam, too, had a daughter and brought their baby girl to America as well. They later had a son.

Judy and Helen and their families came to Denver, a city that in the 1940s was short on experienced tailors. Judy owned a tailor shop and dry-cleaning store, and Helen worked as a tailor for a department store for more than three decades. Over the years they both donated their time to speak to schools and community groups about their experiences.

"To us, America was the land of milk and honey. Remember how lucky you are to be here."

THOMAS TOIVI BLATT

AUTHOR, LECTURER, RETIRED BUSINESSMAN, CHAIRMAN OF THE HOLOCAUST SITES
PRESERVATION COMMITTEE & SURVIVOR OF THE DEATH CAMP, SOBIBOR

Some Holocaust survivors want to wash their hands of the nightmares and memories. Not Thomas Blatt. His goal is to set the record straight.

Blatt experienced the Nazi persecution in many ways. He was forced into a ghetto, escaped, and lived on forged Catholic ID papers outside the ghetto walls. Discovered, he was jailed and later sent to the death camp, Sobibor. After the revolt and escape, he hid in the forest. In a surprise attack, anti-Semites shot Thomas. Although a bullet entered his head, he feigned death and survived. Later, he fought with the resistance forces of the Polish underground until the end of the war. Time and again, he escaped; he survived.

Blatt's first escape was from the ghetto in his hometown of Izbica. In the fall of 1942, posing as a Christian, Thomas tried to escape to Hungary. En route, his train passed Belzec, another death camp in Poland designed exclusively for exterminating Jews. Seeing the flames light the night sky as his train passed, Blatt realized what fate he was escaping. He was discovered as a Jew on the train and was imprisoned, but managed to escape and return to Izbica. A short time later, the Izbica ghetto was liquidated, and he and his family were taken to the death camp, Sobibor. His family was immediately gassed to death, but he was selected to work there as a shoe-shine boy for the Nazis.

In Sobibor, Thomas became an active conspirator in the Sobibor underground organization. On October 14, 1943, the group led a revolt and mass escape. They overpowered the camp guards and seized the armory. The revolt resulted in the death of nearly all the Nazi staff and enabled more than 300 prisoners to escape into the

"Normal people perpetrated the Holocaust ... and the world must understand how very delicate the crust of our civilization and culture is ... because with the right economic and political circumstances, the Holocaust could happen again. This is a warning to all humanity."

forest. It was the most successful revolt and escape in any German camp during World War II. Blatt is one of the few people of the Sobibor Uprising still alive today.

Blatt and two fellow prisoners escaped to a farm near Izbica. After a while, the farmer unexpectedly turned on them, presumably for money, and shot all three. Thomas was left for dead with a bullet in his jaw and escaped again. Next, under the guise of a Catholic Pole, he fought in the Polish underground against the Nazis until liberation.

Thomas immigrated to America in 1959. He was disheartened to learn people in America, and even in Israel, were ignorant about Sobibor. "This is some fantasy," a fellow survivor and Israeli book publisher once told Blatt. Finally, Blatt's story was told in the film *Escape from Sobibor.* That 1987 Globe Award–winning film tells the story of the brave prisoners of Sobibor.

Today, Blatt is guided by a single, burning mission. He continues writing, lecturing, and traveling the world to repeatedly tell the story of Jewish resistance. It is largely through his efforts that a great deal of evidence about Sobibor has been published and the fate of the Jews at this camp brought to light.

In 1992, Thomas Blatt almost single-handedly prevailed upon the Polish authorities to correct a historical lie and remove the tablet displayed at Sobibor. The tablet falsely stated that the primary victims of Sobibor were non-Jewish Russian prisoners of war, Gypsies, and Poles. This was the first time that such an important correction was made in countries formerly behind the Iron Curtain. Without his sustained and constant pressure on the Polish government, few would know that Jews—a quarter of a million Jews—were the only victims at the camp.

DAVID BRAM

BUSINESSMAN, ENTREPRENEUR, COMMUNITY VOLUNTEER & SURVIVOR OF POZNAN, BRESLAU,
GROSS-ROSEN, AUSCHWITZ-BIRKENAU, AND EBENSEE CONCENTRATION CAMPS

David Bram is the only member of his family to survive the Holocaust. The tattered Torah scroll he holds is all that is left of an extinct Jewish community in Europe.

Bram was born in Rusiec, a small town in southwest Poland. He was the eldest of six children and lived in a two-room house with his parents, Mendel and Leah Bram; grandparents, Rifka and Abraham Friedman; brothers, Baruch, Yitzhak, Moishe, and Mordechai; and his sister, Figa. In 1940, the Nazis herded Bram, who was then 13, and his family to the town of Zelow where the men were rounded up for work. David volunteered to work in place of his father, leaving his elder behind to provide for the family. He never saw any of them again.

For two years, Bram worked in labor camps in Poznan, Breslau, and Gross-Rosen. In 1943, he was sent to Auschwitz-Birkenau. David remembers the "sorting" upon his arrival at Birkenau. "The SS said anyone not able to walk, step to the left. Everyone else step to the right. They said there was a three-mile hike to the barracks. I went to the left because I was tired. People were being loaded into trucks. I didn't know it, but they were to be taken to the gas chambers. One SS man got hold of me, kicked me in the rear, and threw me to the other side."

From Auschwitz, Bram was sent to a sub-camp of Mauthausen in Ebensee, Austria. He worked in the mines, enduring subzero cold in his cotton uniform. He and several other prisoners took a blanket off a dead man, tore it into strips, and wrapped it around their legs under their prison garb. That night, betrayed to the SS by a "kapo" (concentration camp overseer), the men were stripped and lined up outside. One by one, they were beaten to death by two SS guards. David was the last in line. The officer kicked him and sent him back to the barracks.

The Germans abandoned the camp in the middle of the night on May 3, 1945, and the U.S. Army liberated it on May 5. "When the Americans came, everyone was just crying and hollering, and people were dying everywhere," Bram says. He weighed 80 pounds.

David Bram immigrated to America in 1947. He married, and he and his wife raised four children. They now have seven grandchildren. Bram developed a number of successful businesses and also became a real estate developer. He helped build his community's synagogue and has volunteered many hours to support the State of Israel. He regularly speaks to school and community groups about his experiences.

Through the years since his liberation, Bram has searched the world over with hope that he might find a relative alive. He has not. But in 1989, he brought a symbolic piece of his past home. David obtained a Torah scroll that had been confiscated by the Nazis from a synagogue in Czechoslovakia. Hundreds of Torah scrolls had been collected, intended to become part of a permanent Nazi exhibition as relics of a defunct culture. Later, the scrolls were entrusted to a synagogue in London, where they have been loaned to synagogues and educational institutions throughout the world.

David brought Scroll No. 152 back to his community in Colorado Springs and dedicated it in memory of his family—a memorial to the vanished communities of Europe and a gift to future generations. "Take this Torah," he tells the children of his community. "Take it to heart. Learn from it and from the stories it holds."

"Never give up hope.

I told myself more

than once that as long

as my heart beats,

I will never give up."

SELENE BRUK

HOLOCAUST EDUCATOR & SURVIVOR OF THE BIALYSTOK GHETTO AND STUTTHOF, AUSCHWITZ-BIRKENAU, RAVENSBRÜCK, AND NEUSTADT CONCENTRATION CAMPS

These Jews, they were here!" said an angry SS officer who entered the room where Selene Bruk and her family were hiding. Bruk was hiding under a bed and could see the reflection of her face in the officer's polished boots. "My heart was racing. I prayed he wouldn't look down."

Bruk and her family were hiding from the SS as the ghetto of Bialystok was being liquidated. Bialystok was Bruk's hometown and also home to 60,000 other Jews. When Germany and the Soviet Union divided Poland in 1939, the city came under Soviet occupation.

In 1941, Germany invaded Soviet-occupied Poland. Two thousand Jewish men were burned alive in Bialystok's main synagogue. As the city burned, people ironically were able to escape death in the cemetery, one of the few places not in flames.

Thousands of Jews were periodically taken from the ghetto. Soldiers said the Jews were being taken to other cities to work. Instead, they were being murdered. Bruk remembers hiding during the SS roundups in the ghetto. "We hid in the attic and listened to the killing and shooting outside."

Selene was arrested in one roundup and thrown in jail with 200 other teenage girls. Her brother convinced the Germans that she was needed on a construction project. All the other girls were killed. Bruk's uncle and grandfather were taken away in another selection.

After the Bialystok ghetto was liquidated, Selene, her brother, and her mother remained in hiding for three months. Each night, Bruk's brother would rummage for flour and collect water from toilets. They were discovered by a Pole, however, who turned Bruk and her mother over to the Germans. Her brother escaped to the forest and joined the partisans.

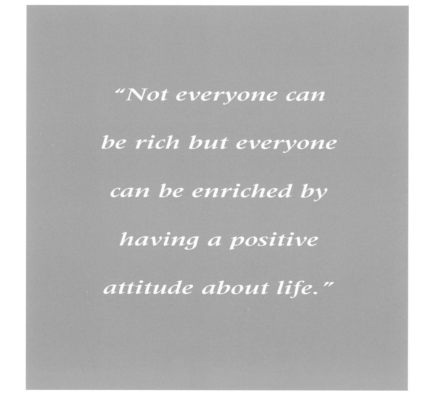

"Not everyone can be rich but everyone can be enriched by having a positive attitude about life."

Selene and her mother were sent to the Stutthof concentration camp for two months and then on to Auschwitz. Bruk watched as the selections began. A soldier shouted out "Right!" or "Left!" as he inspected the prisoners. Bruk saw that her mother was sent to the line of those who were sick and elderly, so she pushed her mother into the other line, saving her life.

They were both sent to Birkenau where they worked for a year in an armaments factory. Out her window, Bruk could see the chimney of the crematorium. "Day after day, I heard the transports arriving. I looked at the chimney and it was a red flame—like a red tongue reaching up to the sky, and I wondered which of my cousins, my grandparents, my aunts, my uncles—who, I asked, was going through that chimney now?"

When the Soviet Army approached, Germans forced the inmates on a week-long death march to Germany. She and her mother survived the march and two more camps, Ravensbrück and Neustadt.

Bruk and her mother were liberated by the Soviets in May 1945. They then returned to Poland to search for family. Selene found letters from her father who was living in America. Her brother was in the Soviet Army. She returned to Germany and had intended to immigrate to the United States. On a train, she met Barry Bruk, a survivor from Lodz. They were married in Montreal in 1950, the same year Bruk graduated from high school. They now live in the United States.

Selene Bruk has two children and five grandchildren. She is the longtime chairperson of a committee for the Anti-Defamation League in Los Angeles that conceived of and engineered the League's model Holocaust education workshop. She frequently speaks about her experiences to school and community groups and is also involved with other Jewish organizations.

LIDIA BUDGOR

BUSINESSWOMAN, HUMANITARIAN, COMMUNITY VOLUNTEER & SURVIVOR
OF THE LODZ GHETTO AND AUSCHWITZ AND STUTTHOF CONCENTRATION CAMPS

This woman was stolen from the jaws of death again and again; sometimes because of whom she knew, sometimes because of the way she looked, and sometimes it was just luck. Each time, Lidia Budgor survived.

Budgor, born Lidia Gryngras, was 14 when the Nazis invaded Poland. "I remember so vividly the infamous Friday night, September 1, 1939, when the German planes circled the skies over Lodz, Poland, dropping bombs over our roofs. I remember the fear and destruction. I found myself in the Lodz ghetto with my parents, two little brothers, two little sisters, and two aunts—all living in one room. Sickness, hunger, and freezing days and nights prevailed. Still, I was filled with hope for better days to come. We were still together."

Within a month of those first bombs, the Germans had confiscated her family's business, a silk thread company. Budgor would try to steal extra food at her job in the ghetto's food distribution center—taking an extra potato or hiding pieces of horse fat in her armpits. She was caught by the Nazis. Her family's high-placed connections with the ghetto's ruling council saved the young girl from her sentence, to be a human dray animal hauling cesspool waste.

Every week, her family received "selection" slips, calling them to be sent to a Nazi labor camp. Again, her influence with ghetto officials got the slips rescinded. In 1942, everyone in the ghetto was told that all their children, five years of age or under, had been selected for children's camps. The children were to be transported in the morning. "Can you imagine what was going on that night in the ghetto? There was crying, screaming, and praying to God that something would happen—even that bombs would fall. This is how bad it was."

In August 1944, the Lodz ghetto was liquidated. Her family was hidden for a short time but soon was picked up by the Nazis. Her father was put in one van with other men. The rest of the family was put on a streetcar. "A Jewish policeman who knew us pulled us off that streetcar. We never saw my father again." A few weeks later, she and the remaining members of her family were sent to Auschwitz.

"I can still see the frightened eyes of my littler sisters and brothers, all cramped together in the cattle cars on the way to Auschwitz. I see them all—the little children, so hungry, hurrying out from the boxcars, bewildered—soldiers, rifles, guns, dogs, and screams....We already knew our fate. My little sister asked, 'Tell me, will it hurt me?' My brother ran over and kissed our mother, whom he loved so very much. This was the end of my family. I never saw them again. So many years have passed, and I still see the frightened eyes of my little sisters and brothers upon separation at Auschwitz."

Unlike the rest of her family, Lidia was spared the gas chambers. Because of her beauty and features, she continued to win favors and special treatment. She was transferred to Stutthof, contracted typhus, survived a six-week winter death march, and weighed just 80 pounds. She was liberated in March 1945. "I remember those days after the war—the terrible loneliness—riding the open freight trains to Lodz, wandering the streets, looking for loved ones, not wanting to believe that all was lost."

Lidia Budgor married a fellow Stutthof survivor, immigrated to the United States in 1952, and raised a family. She runs a successful fashion boutique, and donates countless hours speaking to students about her Holocaust experience. "The survivors have a moral obligation to always remember the blackest years of the Holocaust," she says. "The world is still not free of the sick minds that led to Auschwitz and so many other death camps. Each of us fought, if not with force, always with spirit. We must leave the legacy of remembering the past and warn the world not to let it happen again."

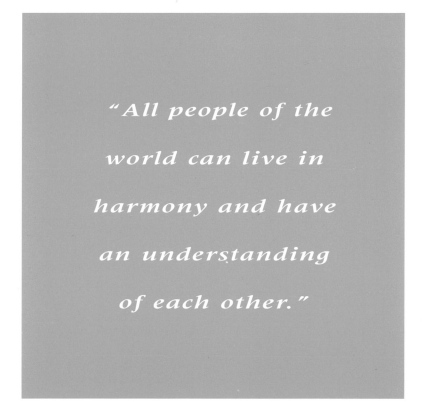

"All people of the world can live in harmony and have an understanding of each other."

25

DAVID T. CHASE

ENTREPRENEUR, NATIONAL AND INTERNATIONAL BUSINESS EXECUTIVE,
PHILANTHROPIST & SURVIVOR OF AUSCHWITZ AND MAUTHAUSEN CONCENTRATION CAMPS

David T. Chase, born David Ciesla, was marching with his father. They were prisoners in the Nazi concentration and death camp, Auschwitz, and were on a death march to Sachsenhausen, Germany, near Berlin. The year was 1943. The Nazi occupation had separated his once-prosperous family of five. Most of them were sent to various Nazi camps. As 14-year-old David marched, exhausted and malnourished, he collapsed. He never saw his father again.

Two years later, David marched again, this time on a death march from Mauthausen, a Nazi camp in Austria, to the gas chambers. The line of prisoners moved through the forest. He watched many ahead of him stumble from the path, only to be shot in the head by the Nazis and left for dead. He decided to take his chances. David jumped in a trench, fell to his stomach, and buried his face in the ground. He waited for a shot to ring out, but there was no bullet. Chase took cover in the woods and the U.S. Army discovered him five days later.

He made his way back to his hometown in Poland to search for his more than 50 relatives. He found an aunt and cousin, and later, a sister, who had been hidden during the war by a Catholic friend. It was his sister who persuaded him to immigrate to America to get an education and begin life anew.

David vividly recalls his entrance to New York Harbor in 1946. He passed the Statue of Liberty with a "Displaced Persons" tag on his clothing and 25 cents in his pocket. He was 17 years old. He immigrated with the help of the United Jewish Appeal, an organization to which he continues to show his generosity. Humbly grateful for his new homeland, Chase is a proud and patriotic American. "America gave us a home when we had none," he says. "America embraced us when we felt rejected.... The initials *DP* that identified us as Displaced Persons ... years ago have taken on a new meaning. Today, the letters *DP* identify us as Delayed Pilgrims. We are proud to be Americans."

David Chase's life since liberation is the embodiment of the American dream. He was educated at Hillyer College and the University of Connecticut. He began work as a door-to-door salesman. Then, he quickly progressed to become the founder of a discount department store that helped him earn his first million dollars by the age of 27. Since then, Chase Enterprises has diversified into real estate, media, and investments, both in the United States and abroad, and boasts a net worth of at least half a billion dollars.

Among his many investments, he is noted as a leading partner in the establishment of Poland's first cable system.

Equally impressive as his business successes are his philanthropic efforts. Along with his charitable contributions to dozens of educational institutions, David Chase is one of the largest contributors to the Jewish Federation. He is a founder of, and a million-dollar donor to, the U.S. Holocaust Memorial Museum in Washington, D.C. At the same time, he is the man who donated a house near his home for use as a Buddhist temple, is a trustee to the Foundation for the Advancement of Catholic Schools, donates to the United Negro College Fund, and grants 100 scholarships to local job training programs in every city in which he builds.

David Chase tells others, "Do philanthropy for the good of it. The ultimate goal is to make the world a better place to live." His accumulation of wealth has merely been a means to that end. He once said, "I needed money to do what I wanted to do: to build a future, and do good with it."

> *"This is the time to challenge the world ... it is yours. Don't ever put artificial restrictions on yourself. Don't wait for something to drop in your lap or for other people to motivate you—try it."*

SIMON CHESTER

RETIRED DIAMOND BROKER & SURVIVOR OF THE LODZ GHETTO
AND AUSCHWITZ-BIRKENAU AND GLEIWITZ CONCENTRATION CAMPS

He went from a prosperous Polish family to the Polish Army, to the ghetto, and to the camps, but he did not go to his death. Simon Chester was born in 1916 under the name of Szlama Czestochowski. He was the son of a textile industrialist in Lodz, but the war changed everything.

Chester was drafted into the Polish Army in 1938. He was on the border between Poland and Germany when the Nazis moved into his hometown of Lodz. He was also among Polish forces when the city of Warsaw fell to the Nazis on September 27, 1939. Polish fighters defending the city did not know of the surrender and only learned of it from their enemies. "Polish soldiers were informed by the Nazis to lay down their arms and get passes to return home. But when I went to get a pass, I found out it was all a trick. Instead, I was arrested as a prisoner of war and was to be sent to Germany as a slave laborer. I managed to escape and returned to Lodz."

In 1940, the Jews of Lodz were forced into the ghetto. Chester and his family endured starvation and abuse for nearly four years. His mother, who was very ill, could not get proper medical attention in the ghetto and died in 1942. The rest of the family stayed in the ghetto and in August 1944 were deported to the death camp at Auschwitz-Birkenau as part of the liquidation of the Lodz ghetto.

"When faced with adversity, people with solid values and strong character do not abandon their integrity, sensitivity, and perspective on life."

Simon's father, Berish Czestochowski, was then 60 years old—too old to be considered "useful" by the Germans. He was sent to the gas chambers upon his arrival at the camp. Chester and his younger brother Samuel were sent to a labor camp at Gleiwitz. Because of a slight infection, 19-year-old Samuel was sent back to Birkenau and gassed to death.

Simon continued living in a Nazi labor camp, working as a riveter on damaged railroad cars. In January 1945, he and thousands of other prisoners began a forced death march from Poland to Germany. Knowing the brutal march would kill him, Chester escaped. He made his way back to Lodz. He later learned his older brother Yechil had starved to death in another concentration camp, and his sister-in-law was murdered at Stutthof, a death camp near Danzig. He had lost his entire family in the Holocaust.

Simon Chester came to the United States to start his life over. He landed a job in the textile business. Later, he befriended a man in New York City who agreed to teach him the diamond business. Chester's successful career as a diamond broker took him to diamond centers around the world. Now retired, Chester says his most important jewels are his family and his grandchildren. "They're all very, very precious."

ROBERT CLARY

ENTERTAINER, ACTOR & SURVIVOR OF BLECHHAMMER,
GROSS-ROSEN, AND BUCHENWALD CONCENTRATION CAMPS

Humility is often more important than fame. Robert Clary has both. Clary was born the youngest of 14 children in Paris, France. Born as Robert Widerman, Clary was 12 years old when he began to fulfill his dream of being an actor, singing in nightclubs throughout Paris.

When he was 16, Clary was taken from his family and shipped off to a concentration camp. Between 1942 and 1945, he was in two transit camps, Drancy in France and another camp in Germany, and also survived the Blechhammer, Gross-Rosen, and Buchenwald concentration camps. When he was liberated on April 11, 1945, he was the only member of his family still alive. "Somehow I survived and emerged from Buchenwald. And when I did, I vowed never to stand by silently and permit evil an easy victory. It has not been difficult for me to keep this promise in mind. Every time I learn of another incident of the vicious hatred of anti-Semitism, I recall personal memories that are almost too painful to bear. But I am also reminded of what I must do."

After the war, Robert returned to France and continued working in nightclubs. Clary's entertainment talents were soon discovered by an American in 1947 in a Paris club. He was singing "Put Your Shoes on Lucy," a song that catapulted him to stardom in the United States where it was an immediate hit recording. "Who would have thought, when my life was dependent on the whim of the SS whether I lived or died while in the concentration camps, that I would have such joyous years and see my childhood dream come true," he said.

Clary's nightclub performances led him to acting work in theater, motion pictures, and television. His acting credits include Broadway shows, motion pictures, and scores of nightclub and television appearances. For decades, Robert has appeared in American soap operas including "The Young and the Restless," "Days of Our Lives," and "The Bold and the Beautiful." The role he is most identified with is that of Louis Lebeau, the Frenchman on "Hogan's Heroes," a first-run comedy series about a German prison camp. The popular series ran on U.S. network television for six years, and now can be seen almost any day on reruns both nationally and around the world.

"Working as an actor lets me play many roles," he says. "But none is more crucial than the real-life role I play ... speaking to countless young audiences about my experiences and about the crucial importance of fighting the rising anti-Semitic tide." Since 1980, Clary has volunteered for the Simon Wiesenthal Center, making some 150 speeches a year in the United States and Canada, reaching approximately 150,000 people. He says his most important educational effort is an outreach program to high schools about the Holocaust.

Today, Robert's other passion is creating carefree and peaceful street scenes from his trips around the world. Using colored pencils, he painstakingly creates detailed images of people of all ages and from all walks of life. Clary scoffs at the commercial value of his art, and says he simply loves to paint. His artful images are a stark contrast to the darker days of his youth that he hopes will never return.

"If this evil should ever again triumph, it will not be because *I* did nothing," Robert Clary says. "My wish is that a hundred years from now, when a teacher asks a student to face a map of the world, to close his eyes and point to a place on the map ... when that child opens his eyes, wherever he has pointed, that place in the world will be at peace ... no wars, no famine, no hatred."

> *"I beg the next generation not to do what people have done for centuries—hate others because of their skin, shape of their eyes, or religious preference. I know what hatred does. I barely escaped what hatred does."*

RALPH CODIKOW

MACHINE SHOP OWNER & SURVIVOR OF THE KOVNO GHETTO AND LANDSBERG, DACHAU, AUSCHWITZ-BIRKENAU, AND BUCHENWALD CONCENTRATION CAMPS

The year was 1941. Codikow was 11 years old when Germans took control of his village of Panemune near Kovno, Lithuania. Conditions for Jews there had already become bad. With anti-Semitism rampant, Lithuanians killed many Jews before the Germans ever arrived. The Codikow family was arrested, and the men were separated from the women. Because of his age, Ralph went with his mother. That day, his grandfather and brother, along with thousands of Lithuanian Jewish men, were shot. Later, Ralph's father was shot, too. He left behind his papers and war medals from his service in the Lithuanian Army.

Within a month, Codikow and his mother were forced into the Kovno ghetto. Each worked a job in the ghetto, but there was little to eat. Ralph would barter for food with the Lithuanians through the barbed-wire fence. It was not without risk and often unproductive. Once, Codikow traded his jacket for a package of butter, only to find that the wrappings held a clay brick.

Twice, he was saved from certain death in the ghetto: once, when his mother used his father's war medals to get Codikow released from a group of "selected" prisoners destined for the concentration camps, and again when his boss in the pottery factory where he worked convinced soldiers that Codikow was crucial to the factory's operation. In 1944, Ralph and his mother were put on a train destined for the camps. The train first stopped at Stutthof, where the women were separated from the men. It was the last time Codikow saw his mother. He later learned that she died there during the last days of the war.

Ralph was sent on to Landsberg and then on to Dachau. After a week, he, along with 130 other children, was placed in a train car to be transported to Auschwitz. Codikow knew what would happen there, and tried to help save any lives he could. Codikow and others devised a plan to distract the guards as some of the boys escaped, then, many miles later, reported the missing boys to the Nazis. Ralph knew that a successful escape meant punishment or death for those left behind, but the plan worked. The children on the train went unpunished because they reported the escape as though it had just happened.

Instead of being sent to the gas chambers, Codikow was now a prisoner at Auschwitz. One morning during roll call, Nazi officers were asking the children their ages. Ralph was now 14, but he saw that when the boy in front of him, also 14, gave his true age, the officer wrote down the boy's number. When it was Ralph's turn, he told the officer that he was 15 and the officer took no notes. Later that day, the boys whose numbers had been written down were taken away and never seen again.

Codikow again escaped death in Buchenwald. He hid with a group of young Russian prisoners, while dozens of other children were marched into a field and shot. Not long after his clever maneuver, American soldiers arrived to liberate the camp.

Ralph Codikow immigrated to the United States and owned and operated an advanced, high-performance tool and die business. That had been his lifelong dream, that and a few simple pleasures: a loving family, control over his destiny, and being a respected employer. "Anything more," Codikow said, "would be too much." Ralph died in October 1995. He believed strongly in educating people about the Holocaust, especially those who have dismissed the Holocaust as fiction.

"Faith and hope are strong emotions ... through this horrible time in history—faith and hope have enabled us to survive."

FREDDY DIAMENT

RETIRED BUSINESSMAN, COMMUNITY LEADER & SURVIVOR OF
SACHSENHAUSEN AND AUSCHWITZ CONCENTRATION CAMPS

"Long live liberty!" These three words have been seared into Freddy Diament's memory. His older brother, Leo, pierced the silence with those words as a hangman's noose was being placed around his neck on the gallows at Auschwitz in October 1944. His brother and two friends were members of the secret underground at Auschwitz that sought to sabotage the extermination plans of the SS.

The three inmates had been betrayed by a fellow prisoner and sentenced to death for planning a mass breakout at the concentration camp. Diament was one of the 10,000 Jewish prisoners who witnessed the hangings.

In his written account of the hangings, Diament remembers the voice of one of the guards: "'In the name of the German people and on behalf of the Reichsfuehrer SS Himmler … Death by Hanging.' Seconds of icy and torpid silence follow. The 10,000 slaves hold their breath. And then, like thunder, a loud and clear voice from the gallows cuts the silence and carries over the parade ground: 'Courage, Comrades! We are the last victims!' (yells the first to be hanged) … The crate is pulled away under (the next victim's) feet. As the body is swinging freely, the hangman pulls the feet … to hasten the death…. Leo, the youngest of the three, mounts the crate. As the hangman approaches, his voice rings out and carries through the air and into our hearts: 'Es—lebe—die—Freiheit!' (Long live liberty!) The 10,000 are stirred to the depth of their souls. The SS guards stand as if they had turned into stone. We feel proud again of being Jews."

Until that moment, Freddy and his brother had survived five years in the camps. Together with their father, they were arrested by the Gestapo in September 1939. They were incarcerated in the Sachsenhausen concentration camp for three years. In 1942, they were deported to Auschwitz where his father was beaten to death by the SS.

In 1945, Diament participated in the Death March of Auschwitz, when 75,000 inmates were forced to walk from Poland to Germany, going weeks with little food or drink. Although weak and emaciated, Freddy escaped the march and worked for the underground forces until the end of the war.

He was an organizer of the first ship illegally carrying 1,200 Holocaust survivors to Palestine through the British blockade. In Israel, he was a founding member of Kibbutz-Buchenwald (later renamed in Hebrew, *Netzer-Sereni*), the first kibbutz established by survivors in 1946. Between 1956 and 1966, Diament testified seven times in war crimes trials in Germany. To a large degree, it was his testimony that resulted in the conviction of six SS guards of the Sachsenhausen and Auschwitz camps.

After immigrating to the United States, Freddy attended night classes for 11 years and earned a BS and an MBA degree from California State University in Los Angeles. Today, he is a retired manufacturer of women's high-fashion clothing. Freddy Diament works on behalf of survivors and other Jewish causes without pause. He has been awarded the Jerusalem Peace Prize by the State of Israel Bonds organization; he helped plan both the World Gathering of Jewish Holocaust Survivors in Israel in 1981 and the American Gathering of Jewish Holocaust Survivors in Washington, D.C., in 1983; he has served such organizations as the U.S. Holocaust Memorial Museum in Washington, D.C., the Jewish Federation Council, the Bureau of Jewish Education, the Jewish Television Network, and more; and he is a founder of the Hebrew University in Jerusalem, Ben Gurion University of the Negev in Israel, and the University of Judaism in Los Angeles.

"No one is an island unto themselves. Everything in life affects us all."

Max Drimmer & Herman Shine

Boyhood Friends & Survivors of Sachsenhausen and Auschwitz Concentration Camps

These men share an extraordinary relationship. They shared their childhoods, were arrested together as teenagers at the start of World War II, escaped Auschwitz together, were saved together by a Polish Catholic, married together, and then came to America together. In 1989, they completed their story together, as they found and met the man who had saved their lives 50 years earlier.

Max Drimmer and Herman Shine grew up in Berlin. They had known each other as small children. When the war broke out in 1939, Drimmer was 19 and Shine nearly 17. They were both arrested for being Jewish and were sent to the Sachsenhausen concentration camp near Berlin. There they were imprisoned for three years before being sent to Auschwitz for another two years.

Shine worked as a roofer in the camp. Drimmer was forced to work at the nearby I.G. Farben factory, where the Zyklon B gas used in the death chambers was manufactured. It was there that Josef Wrona, a Polish Catholic, was working as a civilian employee.

Drimmer and Wrona became surreptitious friends. Wrona would sometimes smuggle a slice of bread or a cigarette to Drimmer. When Wrona overheard a conversation between two SS guards about the planned murder of all the Auschwitz prisoners, he offered to hide Drimmer. "Will you take my friend, too?" Drimmer asked.

Wrona dug a pit next to a wall in a warehouse on the factory grounds. There he hid the two men, and covered the pit with insulation material. In darkness, the men emerged from the pit, crawled on their bellies under the barbed wire, and ran through the night, evading the Nazis several times as they headed toward the village of Nowa Wies. Drimmer and Shine were to have been met by resistance leaders who were going to take them the rest of the way to the partisans. They waited for the resistance fighters in vain.

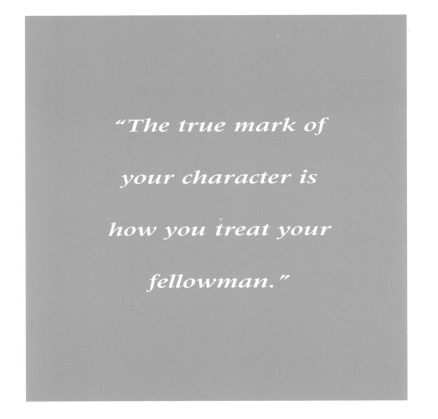

"The true mark of your character is how you treat your fellowman."

For the next four months, the pair hid in a barn behind Wrona's farmhouse. Wrona fed them from his own meager rations. By hiding Jews, he put his life and the lives of his family in danger. In one incident, the Gestapo intercepted a letter to Max from his sweetheart, Herta, whom he later married. The next day, the Gestapo arrived with dogs to sniff out Max and Herman. Undetected, the pair, who had been hiding in the hayloft, then fled to the parents' home of Herman's wife-to-be, Marianne, whom he had met previously in the Gleiwitz concentration camp.

When the war ended, Drimmer and Shine came out of hiding and returned to Berlin. Both discovered that their families had been killed.

The young men married in a double wedding at the Berlin city hall and brought their brides to America. They settled in California and each prospered—Drimmer as a plumbing contractor and Shine as a roofing contractor. All the while, they wondered about and searched for the man who had helped them escape the infamous extermination camp. Despite their best efforts, including return trips to Poland, the pair could not find Wrona. Then, a documentary filmmaker accompanied the two men to Eastern Europe and located a veteran of the Polish underground who had access to information about Wrona. When the friends learned of Wrona's whereabouts, they sent for him.

Wrona came to visit them in the United States in 1990. He stayed for five weeks. Then in his late sixties, the retired bookkeeper from Europe was received by the California legislature, bestowed by a representative of Yad Vashem with the medal of a "Righteous Gentile," and showered with hugs, kisses, and parties. Wrona said his actions were simply fulfilling a human obligation. Max and Herman remained in touch with Josef Wrona until he passed away in November 1990.

Today, they lecture in local schools to fulfill their obligation of ensuring that those who were not as lucky as they are not forgotten.

וסנה איננו אכל

Remember
the Shoah Holocaust

FRED ENGLARD

INDUSTRIAL FABRICS SPECIALIST, COMMUNITY VOLUNTEER, HOLOCAUST SPEAKER & SURVIVOR OF THE LODZ GHETTO AND AUSCHWITZ AND SIEGMAR-SCHOENAU CONCENTRATION CAMPS

Raus! Raus!" yelled the German guards. "Women over here! Men this way!... Right, left, right!" That is how Fred Englard lost his mother and father. There were no good-byes on the selection platform at Auschwitz. That is where the Nazis separated those destined to die from the able-bodied prisoners. Women who refused to leave their small children, the ill, and the elderly were all immediately sent to their deaths. There were no burials, no tombstones, no chance to say Kaddish, the Hebrew prayer for the dead. Englard learned from fellow prisoners that his parents had been sent to the gas chambers upon their arrival at the death camp. A young man in his twenties, Fred was made a slave laborer.

Englard's family was from Lodz, Poland, and they had been there for five generations. His father was successful in the textile industry. Shortly after World War II began, the Jews of Lodz were ordered to assemble and were forced into the barbed-wire-enclosed ghetto. There was no connection with the outside world. Fred's three married sisters had fled to Warsaw in the hopes of better conditions, but all died there at the hands of the Nazis. In 1944, after four years in the ghetto, Englard and his parents were put in railroad cattle cars and sent to Auschwitz.

Ten weeks after his arrival there, an order came down for 400 prisoners to be sent to Germany to work as slave laborers. Englard's barrack was one of those chosen for the detachment. They were sent to the Siegmar-Schoenau labor camp, a sub-camp of the Flossenbürg concentration camp, where the prisoners worked in a variety of German factories. By the spring of 1945, half of Fred's fellow prisoners had died of exposure, malnutrition, beatings, and shootings.

Just before the Allies liberated the camps in 1945, Englard and the other Jews were forced to march day and night. They marched from one city to another because the Nazis did not know what to do with the prisoners. Fred, weakened from malnutrition, summoned all his strength to keep marching. On May 10, 1945, nine days after Hitler perished, Nazis assembled Fred's group at gunpoint in a farm field and declared them free. The SS, fearing recrimination, fled for their lives with their weapons.

Three weeks later, Fred returned to his home in Lodz, and learned that he was the only remaining member of a family of more than 250 people. He discovered that, in addition to the murder of his parents, his three sisters with their husbands and children were all exterminated at the Majdanek death camp.

Fred Englard immigrated to the United States in 1953 and raised his own family. He worked in the industrial fabrics aftermarket, and has remained a vigilant voice from the Holocaust. He is a frequent writer of letters to magazines and newspapers to set the record straight and defend history as he experienced it. The word "Holocaust," he says, has become overused and loosely defined. He prefers the word "Shoah," the Hebrew word for Holocaust to describe the atrocities against the Jews. Englard is a collector of literature about the war and is a voracious reader of historical accounts of the Holocaust. He also is a collector of poignant quotations that somehow, for him, assign meaning to what happened between 1939 and 1945. Among his favorites is the following quotation by a fellow Holocaust survivor and scholar, the late Primo Levi.

"If you wish to find the spark in our life, look in the ashes."

VERA FEDERMAN

COMMUNITY LEADER, VOLUNTEER & SURVIVOR OF AUSCHWITZ
AND ALLENDORF-BUCHENWALD CONCENTRATION CAMPS

Vera Federman and her parents listened each night to radio reports on the BBC. They impatiently awaited the entry of the United States into the war as the Germans began their occupation of Hungary and the destruction of its Jews. It was March 1944 and Vera was afraid. "We tried to reassure each other that perhaps the Jews wouldn't be the main target of the invasion." Weeks earlier, she heard a radio report in which Hitler said, "You high and mighty Hungarian Jews, beware! Soap will be made of you, too." As the days passed, so did Vera's illusion that the Germans would leave the Jews alone. One edict followed another. Nazis seized their valuables and forced them into a ghetto.

Then Vera Frank, she was still in her teens when the war broke out. She recalls the frightening days in the ghetto of her hometown of Debrecen. "I looked out the window and saw SS soldiers with drawn bayonets. They were demanding money and jewelry. My parents had only their gold wedding bands and I watched with a wrenching heart as my father, who had never removed his in 21 years, tried to remove the ring."

Next the family was taken to a brick factory. "It was then that we found out about D day. The Americans had finally landed! We wondered if they were too late for us. In the meantime, the first of three transports was assembled. With each transport, cattle cars took away 4,000 people." Vera's family avoided the first two transports but not the third. "We were to board the cattle cars. My father was the first one aboard and on seeing that it was full of animal litter, he grabbed a broom and started sweeping. He was joined by the sister of my best friend. My father looked at her and said, "Susie, take care of my little girl." It was Vera's 20th birthday, June 27, 1944.

"Believe in the power of the individual to make a difference in this world."

"We arrived in Auschwitz on July 1. An SS officer was directing people to the left and to the right. My father was taken away from us. Then, my mother was sent one direction and I the other. I pleaded with the SS man, 'Please, I am only 13 years old.'" Vera thought that if he believed her, he would not separate them, but he did not relent. "My mother started to walk away, then turned, looking back at me with her velvety brown eyes. That is the image I will carry with me forever."

Vera's parents, aunts, uncles, and most of her cousins were immediately gassed. After six weeks at Auschwitz, Vera was shipped to Allendorf to work in a munitions factory. Also in the transport was the family friend, Susie, who had promised Vera's father that she would look after his daughter. Susie helped Vera get a job as a potato peeler, which allowed her some extra food. In the spring of 1945, the prisoners were ordered on a march. They were liberated by U.S. forces on March 30.

Vera immigrated to America in 1948 and attended the University of Washington in Seattle on a scholarship from the Hillel Foundation. She earned degrees in history and French. Her cousin, Maria Frank Abrams, also survived Auschwitz and also resides in Seattle.

Vera Federman now works to preserve the history of her people. She helped build a Holocaust collection at the Temple De Hirsch Sinai Library; she helped create survivors' testimonies and transcripts at the Washington State Jewish Historical Society Archives, located at the University of Washington. She is currently vice president and chair of the Archives Committee of the Surviving Generations of the Holocaust. Vera married and raised two children.

RENEE FIRESTONE

RETIRED FASHION DESIGNER & SURVIVOR OF THE UNGVAR GHETTO
AND AUSCHWITZ AND LIEBAU CONCENTRATION CAMPS

If hell ever had a colony on earth, it was certainly at Auschwitz," wrote Renee Firestone. Her memory of Auschwitz is a wash of "pain, hunger, thirst, cold, heat, hearing sounds too frightening to imitate, seeing sights too terrible to describe, and the smell—the offensive odor of the smoke belching from four tall chimneys."

Firestone was born Renee Weinfeld in Užhorod, Czechoslovakia. She and her family arrived at Auschwitz in 1944 from the Ungvar ghetto in Hungary. The 4,000 Jews of Ungvar had been forced into a one-block area where they were held for three weeks. Firestone had been convinced that they would be transported to Germany to work on farms or in factories. She wanted to believe the rumors that if the young worked hard, the older people would be allowed to take care of their homes and watch the children. Renee anxiously awaited the transport. She waited near the front of the line and signaled her parents and sister to join her as the guards began loading people into cattle cars.

For three days and nights they remained packed in the boxcar. "The stench of human waste became nauseating and my throat and lips became parched from lack of water. Seldom did anyone speak. I do not remember participating in any conversations except to lean down and whisper to my mother. She sat crying and moaning near my feet, convinced that this was the end."

As the train stopped, Firestone moved toward the door. "If we were in Germany, I wanted to be the first in line for a job. Whatever they want, I will do the job. We heard the latches being unlocked and then the doors were pushed open. Excited and in a frenzy, I jumped from the train, ready to get in line." The only lines were "selection" lines, separating those who would be enslaved from those who would die.

Once in the camp, Renee smuggled her sister-in-law, Rozsi, into her barrack and watched over her. Rozsi was ill and feverish. Then came a rumor that the Nazis were liquidating Auschwitz because the Russians were advancing toward the camp. Surrounded by SS soldiers armed with machine guns and German shepherds, the inmates set out on a death march to Liebau, another concentration camp near the old Polish-Czech border. Rozsi could walk no more and begged Firestone to let her die. Before collapsing in the snow, she moaned, "I can't fight anymore, Renee. Let me go!" Renee remembers how fellow prisoners pried Rozsi from her arms and dragged her to the side of the road so that the SS wouldn't notice what was happening.

Firestone worked through the winter in a factory in Liebau. She was a foreman in charge of assembling snow chains for German tanks. Secretly, Renee was a master saboteur, rearranging the patterns of links in the chains so that when mounted on tires miles from the factory, they were no good.

Renee Firestone was liberated by the Russians in May 1945. She found her brother, who had joined the Russian partisans, still alive. Her father, too, had survived the war, but died months later of tuberculosis. Her sister and mother perished at Auschwitz.

Renee married a friend of her brother's, Bernard Firestone. They started a family and immigrated to America in 1949. Firestone then launched her career as a fashion designer. In 1952, she received a phone call at her home in Los Angeles. It was Rozsi. She had survived and had also immigrated to America.

"You only betray yourself when you ignore the inner dreams for your life."

Day in, day out, new transports of prisoners cram-
med into cattle wagons
came to the extermination
camps from various parts
of the country.

ANNA & BENNO FISCHER

FOUNDERS OF THE MARTYRS MEMORIAL AND MUSEUM OF THE HOLOCAUST IN LOS ANGELES & SURVIVORS OF SEVERAL GHETTOS AND CONCENTRATION CAMPS

Some people don't experience a single miracle in a lifetime. Anna and Benno Fischer are alive and together today because of many, many miracles.

Anna and Benno were both born in Poland. They fell in love in 1940 in the ghetto of Skierniewice. It was just one of three ghettos that Anna survived, along with her parents and seven siblings. When deportations began in 1942 from the ghettos to the concentration camps, five of her family members were killed, some murdered on the street before ever boarding the infamous railroad cars that carried so many European Jews to their deaths.

Anna and her sister were blond and blue-eyed, and occasionally posed as non-Jews. Her sister was caught and sent to a death camp, and by 1943, only Anna and her mother were still alive. They were caught hiding in an attic, were beaten and tortured, then loaded into boxcars destined for the Majdanek concentration camp.

Unlike most boxcars, this one did not have bars or barbed wire on the small windows. As the train rolled down the tracks, someone began picking up bodies and pushing them through those openings. "I was one of those who flew out into the night." She awoke in a ditch unhurt, and for 15 days walked back to the ghetto.

Anna planned to join the rest of the Jews to await the next deportation. When that deportation came, she was on her way to Stuttgart, Germany, posing as a Polish Aryan slave laborer. She survived the last two years of the war working as a cleaning girl in a hospital and sanitarium. She was liberated by the Americans on Friday the 13th in April 1945. She was the only member of her family to survive.

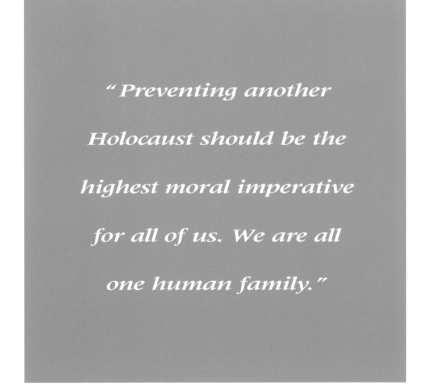

"Preventing another Holocaust should be the highest moral imperative for all of us. We are all one human family."

Benno had just received his diploma from the Architectural School in Warsaw and had been working as an architect for two months when the Germans invaded Poland. He was captured in 1941 and was sent to the first of several camps. Once, a camp leader accused Fischer of slowing down in his work. "He pulled out his pistol and put it in my mouth … I did not feel anything: no fear, no anger, no sorrow. For some reason, he did not pull the trigger. He removed the gun from my mouth and I collapsed. I woke up in my bunk, and my fellow inmates told me how lucky I was to be alive."

Later, Benno was sent to the Flossenbürg concentration camp where he worked in a German plane factory. As the end of the war neared, Benno was one of 5,000 Jewish inmates ordered on a 10-day death march. He was among the few hundred who survived and were liberated in April 1945. He, too, lost his entire family.

Anna and Benno each believed that the other had perished, but they were reunited by a strange coincidence and married in Stuttgart in 1946. That same year, they came to the United States on the first refugee boat from Germany. It docked on May 20, 1946. Benno resumed his architectural practice in Los Angeles, and they raised three children.

In the 1970s, Benno Fischer designed the original Martyrs Memorial and the Museum of the Holocaust in the Jewish Federation Building in Los Angeles, which opened to the public in 1978. Now, he is retired. Anna Fischer is a docent at the museum and conducts tours and lectures there. What Benno designed for that museum, he says, was his tribute to and expression of loyalty to those who perished in the Holocaust.

ABRAHAM FOXMAN

NATIONAL DIRECTOR OF THE ANTI-DEFAMATION LEAGUE & A HIDDEN CHILD OF THE HOLOCAUST

Abraham Foxman was hidden from the Nazis when he was just a boy, but he could not hide from the hatred and horror of the Holocaust. Today his life's mission is to expose hatred and to educate others against it.

Foxman was born in Poland in 1940. He was saved from the Holocaust as an infant by his Polish Catholic nursemaid, who baptized and raised him as a Catholic during the war years. For the first few years of his life, he did not know he was a Jew, nor that his real parents were in Nazi concentration camps. His parents survived, but he lost 14 members of his family. He arrived in the United States in 1950 with his parents after a lengthy custody battle with the former nursemaid, who had come to love him as her own.

Under his father's guidance, Abraham began his Jewish studies. He studied at a Brooklyn, New York, yeshiva, attended college, and earned both a Bachelor of Arts degree and a Juris Doctor's degree. Later, he did graduate work in advanced Judaic studies at the Jewish Theological Seminary. He is fluent in several languages.

Foxman now is America's preeminent spokesperson for the safety and security of the Jewish people, of Israel, and of human rights around the globe. He is the national director of the Anti-Defamation League. Abraham Foxman is respected the world over for his views on domestic and international issues, and his insight is sought by national and world leaders, scholars, and the media. For decades, he has crusaded tirelessly opposing the infectious social ills of anti-Semitism, bigotry, and prejudice.

"We have conquered space and have found an antidote for smallpox. We are capable of doing that which people said is impossible, but we have not found something that will eradicate hate. We must find other means of controlling it, keeping hate unacceptable, intolerable, immoral, and undemocratic. Tolerance," Foxman says, "is the only available social medicine left for mankind.

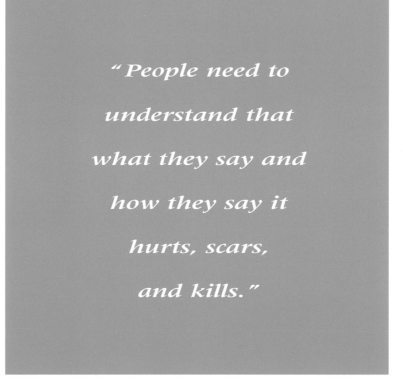

"People need to understand that what they say and how they say it hurts, scars, and kills."

"What is the lesson [of the Holocaust]?" Abraham Foxman asks. "For fifty years, we have focused on the evil that men can do. The further I move from it, the more I begin to try to figure out what is the lesson. The lesson is the *spirit*. I think the lesson of the Holocaust that I want to convey is: Yes, we all know what man is capable of. There is another message and it is the affirmation of life, the affirmation of hope, and the affirmation of faith … To know the hell of the Holocaust and to be willing to survive, to be willing to live another day, to be willing to continue as a human, and to want to live as a Jew … that is the lesson.

"[When I researched the Jewish ghettos,] I could not comprehend how these people could have kindergartens, even though they knew that tomorrow, the kids might be gone. They put on plays and taught the children how to sing songs. That to me is the lesson.

"I want to remember their triumphant spirit—people who affirmed life against all odds, who continued to have faith in humanity despite everything that they saw. In fact, I sit here today because there were people who had courage, who had compassion, who had love, and who had understanding.

"I feel privileged to be doing what I do. What I do every day is very symbolic of what it is that I came from. The experience of hate and love, of deprivation and hope … Embrace good people who care … encourage them to stand up against hate … speak out … reach out … and hold dear that which is good in humanity."

SOLLY GANOR

AUTHOR, MERCHANT MARINE CAPTAIN, TEXTILE BUSINESSMAN
& SURVIVOR OF DACHAU CONCENTRATION CAMP

They had been marching for four days in the cold and the rain. Thousands of prisoners were dying of starvation, exhaustion, and exposure, or they were executed when they could walk no more. Solly Ganor, a Lithuanian-born Jew, was 17 years old.

It was April 1945, and the Nazis were fleeing the advancing Allied armies. Trying to cover up the atrocities they had committed at Dachau, the SS ordered 35,000 prisoners on a death march from the camp to the mountains on the German-Austrian border. There, they were to be executed and their bodies dumped in a lake.

"We marched in silence, a long, grey column of ghostly figures at the end of our endurance. Toward evening, it started to snow. It had soaked through our prison garb, freezing our frail bodies. The SS guards, tired from the long march, were cursing the elements and their superior officers. It was long past rest time, and the order to camp for the night still didn't come. During the last two hours alone, they must have lost more than a thousand prisoners, as they dropped one by one from weakness and exhaustion. Only the dogs were tireless. They snarled and barked as they ran up and down the columns of marching men. They looked for all the world like innocent sheep dogs herding their sheep, but as soon as a prisoner fell, they would begin tearing the fallen man apart. The order finally came to stop. We camped in a clearing in the woods. I found a spot near a tall pine tree. I wrapped myself in my wet blanket, and the falling snow soon covered me. I fell into a deep sleep. During the night, I heard shots all around me as the guards were firing into the sleeping prisoners, but I was too tired to care."

As morning came, Ganor dug himself out of the snow. The noise of the dogs and the gunfire was gone. "There was absolute silence," Solly recalled. "It was as if I was the only one left in the world. Not a soul was in sight, only the white expanse of the snow." The German soldiers had all fled during the night.

Ganor saw a truck carrying four Japanese-American soldiers approach. The soldiers were members of the U.S. Army's much-decorated 522nd Field Artillery Battalion. Before they volunteered for army service, most had been internees themselves in U.S. camps, forced from their homes after Pearl Harbor. Having reached Dachau to liberate it, the soldiers discovered the camp was empty; the crematory ovens were still warm. They followed the 60-mile trail of dead bodies, and came upon Ganor.

Solly will never forget his liberator, Clarence Matsumura. Reaching into his K rations, Matsumura gave Ganor a chocolate bar, assisted him into a vehicle, and drove him to a nearby village. The next day, Ganor was hospitalized. "I never saw Clarence again."

Solly Ganor immigrated to Israel in 1948, where he fought in Israel's War of Independence. After the war, he joined the Merchant Marine where he reached the rank of captain. In 1962, he became manager of a textile factory in Israel, married, raised a family, and spent several years in the United States.

In 1992, Ganor and his liberators were reunited in Israel. In the 50 years since his liberation, Ganor never cried. "I couldn't. I was like an emotional amputee." As he was reunited with Matsumura, there were many, many tears, now recounted in his memoirs, *Light One Candle*. "I felt weak and he was holding me up, just as he did then, 47 years ago in the snow. That event had a profound effect on me. I became a changed person. And I still am." Ganor can cry once again.

"Make sure you're not robbed of your democratic freedoms ... Democracy is as precious as anything can be."

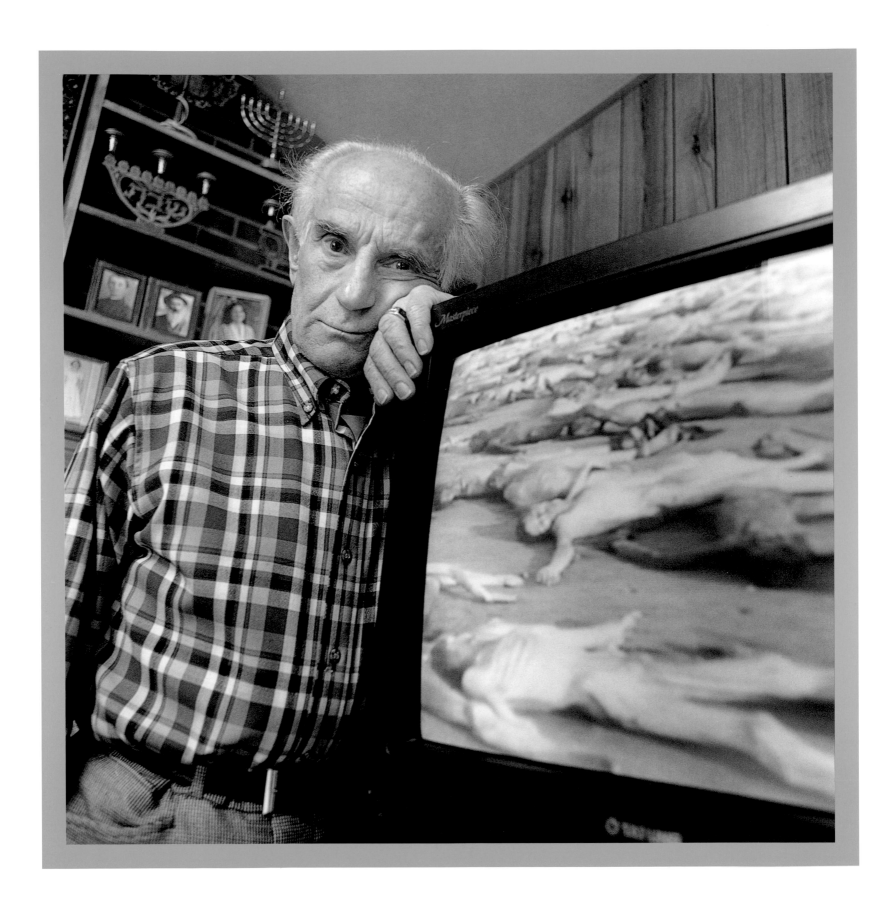

HARRY GLASER

RETIRED CLOTHING RETAILER & SURVIVOR OF AUSCHWITZ, BUCHENWALD, DORA, AND BERGEN-BELSEN CONCENTRATION CAMPS

Harry Glaser and his parents and sister arrived at Auschwitz in 1942. Glaser was 22. Amid the chaos of sorting out which prisoners were to go to the left and which to the right, Glaser persuaded his father to rejoin his mother in the opposite line. "Be together with Mom," he whispered. His father obeyed his son's plea, not realizing they were headed to their deaths in the gas chambers.

Harry and his family were from Romania. His parents had been in the merchandise business.

After he was deported to Auschwitz, Glaser was sent to Buchenwald and then to Dora. From there, he was sent to Bergen-Belsen. He recalled the three-day rail trip to Bergen-Belsen, packed in a boxcar without food or water. Many suffocated and died en route. Glaser was ordered to help stack the dead bodies in another railcar where he was able to breathe and lie down to rest. There among the dead bodies, Harry believes his life was saved. He said he could not have survived the trip if he had remained in the cattle car with the others.

At Bergen-Belsen, Glaser again tended to the dead. He dragged dead bodies by the ankles for burial in mass graves. "I remember the bodies scattered everywhere. There was no food and no water."

On April 15, 1945, as British tanks advanced on Bergen-Belsen, the SS machine-gunned some 25,000 prisoners

"All human beings are precious and should always be treated with respect."

who had stormed the camp gates thinking they were about to be freed. Harry was shot in the leg and lay wounded until British soldiers arrived. Glaser was then liberated along with his sister, Freda. He had not known her whereabouts during the war, but during the liberation of Bergen-Belsen, they were reunited. Freda cleaned his wound and promised she would return with food. Glaser never saw her again and is convinced that she died after eating bread that the SS had laced with rat poison.

The British liberators found thousands of dead bodies at Bergen-Belsen. Mass graves were dug and bulldozers were brought to shovel in the dead. The 60,000 camp prisoners suffered from a typhoid epidemic—so lethal that the camp had to be burned down. An estimated 14,000 of the newly freed inmates died within a few days because their emaciated bodies were unable to respond to medicine or nutrients. British troops took films of Bergen-Belsen that were broadcast throughout the world. In September of that year, 48 Nazis from the Bergen-Belsen camp were tried for their crimes. Eleven, including the camp commandant, were executed.

Harry Glaser immigrated to the United States in December 1947. He lived in New York until he moved west and settled in Denver, Colorado, in the summer of 1954. He is now retired from the retail clothing business.

SAMUEL GOETZ, O.D.

OPTOMETRIST, COMMUNITY LEADER & SURVIVOR OF MAUTHAUSEN AND EBENSEE CONCENTRATION CAMPS

Sam Goetz believes that with knowledge comes truth. That is why he has tirelessly promoted the scholarly study of the Holocaust.

Goetz was 11 years old when the Nazis arrived in his hometown of Tarnow, Poland. Along with other Jews in his town, he was deported to the concentration camps. He spent three years in the camps of Mauthausen and Ebensee and was liberated by the U.S. Army in 1945.

As a teenager, Sam lived in a Displaced Persons (DP) camp in Italy. The DP camps were set up throughout western Europe and were occupied by the American, British, and French forces. DP camps were subsidized by German government and by charitable institutions, the most prominent of which were the United Nations Relief and Rehabilitation Administrations (UNRRA), the American Joint Distribution Committee (JDC), and the Hebrew Immigrant Aid Society (HIAS).

"It was early July 1945 when I arrived in UNRRA camp No. 34 at Santa Maria di Bagni, located at the heel of the Italian boot. UNRRA rations included a pair of underwear, army fatigues, and a pair of socks. Armed with my new possessions, I began my new life as a free man. Each day began with the hope that among newly arriving transports, perhaps a relative would be found, a lost brother or sister, or perhaps a friend or neighbor." Goetz found no family, but he did meet his future wife, Gertrude.

Hope for many survivors came with a directive from President Truman. In December 1945, he mandated preferential treatment for all DPs. In 1948, the "DP Bill" accepted by Congress expanded the original directive and increased immigration quotas. For many like Goetz, immigration to other countries was the only hope for putting their shattered lives together again. "In September of 1949, I embarked on a long trip. I left by train from Naples to Bremerhaven,

> *"We must be dedicated to the difficult past, with a glimpse of hope for a better world for the generations to come."*

Germany, where I finally set sail on the *General CC Balou* to the New World to start a new life," wrote Goetz.

Sam Goetz arrived in New York in 1949. A year later, he joined Gertrude in California. After attending Los Angeles City College at night, Goetz transferred to UCLA. He graduated from the School of Public Health in 1955 and later became an optometrist. He and his wife raised two children. Each family member now holds degrees from UCLA.

In the early 1960s, Sam served as president of The "1939" Club, the largest Holocaust survivors' organization in Los Angeles. In the following decades, he was astounded to find the growing popularity of Holocaust revisionism, an attempt by so-called scholars to call the Holocaust a hoax and to deny the destruction of European Jewry in Nazi concentration camps. "I realized soon enough that unless we, who have personally experienced the events of the Holocaust, respond with vigor to the new revisionism, future generations will hardly learn the true events of the Nazi actions against the Jews in Europe. Education provides the best possible answer to Holocaust revisionism," he says.

Goetz became the driving force to endow a professorship or Chair in Holocaust Studies at UCLA, the first such chair in the United States. That position now forms the nucleus of the University's outstanding Jewish Studies program. Sam was also the driving force behind a video archive recording the testimony of Holocaust survivors, now housed at the University's research library.

Samuel Goetz, a soft-spoken person, is fiercely determined to document and preserve the accuracy of the Holocaust. His one-person crusade to safeguard the future against any possible historical distortions is the legacy he wants to leave for generations to come.

EMIL GOLD & ZESA STARR

BOTH ARE RETIRED FROM THE RETAIL CLOTHING BUSINESS, VOLUNTEERS IN HOLOCAUST EDUCATION & SURVIVORS OF THE CONCENTRATION CAMPS

We came through," said Emil Gold. "How? I don't know how to answer. There is no answer." There are no adequate words or descriptions that explain how and what Emil and his brother Zesa Starr witnessed, endured, and survived during the Nazi Holocaust.

Born in Lubraniec, Poland, Emil and Zesa are the only survivors of an extended family of 26. Between the two of them, they endured 21 concentration camps. During the war, they were separated and spent two years apart, not knowing if the other was dead or alive.

Both ended up in the Poznan labor camp in 1940. There, they were stricken with typhoid fever. In six weeks, recalled Emil, nearly 800 people died. There was no medicine and no water. "People died like flies." Zesa became too sick to work, always a death sentence for camp inmates. He was put on a transport destined for the gas chambers of Auschwitz and Birkenau. "When I heard he was going, I went with him," recalls Emil. "I was not selected to go, but I went with him. Zesa told me not to."

They arrived at Auschwitz-Birkenau where, instead of being selected for death, they were made slave laborers. Standing side by side, they were tattooed with their inmate numbers, 111834 and 111835. Their job was to sort the clothing that was removed from the thousands of people murdered in the gas chambers. "We went through their clothing inch by inch. This was not the way we wanted it, but sometimes we would find some extra food."

They recall how after an especially large transport to Auschwitz, the Nazis killed 60,000 people in the gas chambers in a single night. They recall how a Nazi approached a Hungarian Jew and his three starving sons in the camp and taunted the sons. The Nazi said that if they wanted more food, they should murder their father. The father said, "Kill me, or you will be killed, too"— and they did to get an extra piece of bread. And they recall how in one cell block, where prisoners were sent for punishment, Nazis distributed belts to the prisoners. "Every morning you woke up to find 10 or 20 people had hanged themselves," recalls Emil. "That was what the Germans wanted."

Emil and Zesa endured more camps: Buna, Buchenwald, Weimar, and Bergen-Belsen. En route to one camp, the inmates' train was mistaken for a German military transport and was bombed by the British. Of 1,000 prisoners on the train, 250 lived. Emil, who had been shot in the leg, walked to a Red Cross hospital and was operated on by a German physician whom he credits with saving his life.

Emil was liberated from Bergen-Belsen by British troops on April 15, 1945. The U.S. Army liberated Zesa from Dachau on April 29. Emil began asking others about his brother's fate. By chance, a friend had seen Zesa. Within two weeks, they were reunited. Emil went to Israel and fought for the Israeli underground and in the Israeli Army. Both brothers eventually immigrated to America and are now retired from the retail clothing business. They have settled in Colorado.

Zesa and Emil are grateful beyond words for their children and grandchildren and for the opportunities and freedom they have found in the United States. They speak frequently about the Holocaust in schools, warning young people about the dangers of hate groups. They implore the young to respect and protect the freedoms they have.

> *"Freedom is the most important thing. Enjoy it and live with respect for your fellowman."*

CHAIM GOLDBERG

INTERNATIONALLY ACCLAIMED ARTIST OF THE HOLOCAUST & POW CAMP ESCAPEE AND WAR REFUGEE

His hands fashion memories. Renowned Jewish artist and survivor Chaim Goldberg brings to life a world lost in the horrors of the Holocaust and immortalizes those who fought, those who died, and those who survived.

Goldberg is an artist successful in nearly all mediums, including watercolor, oil, wood, and metal. From portrait-size engravings to his ceiling-high sculptures, Goldberg's work recaptures the warmth and poignancy of the prewar Jewish *shtetl,* or village, in Poland, and the struggles and sufferings of the Holocaust. His renderings are simple in subject—a village wedding, a mother rocking a cradle, a group of worshipers, a ghetto fighter, a prayer—but his interpretation is rich, fluid, almost poetic. His work is in many private collections and in more than 40 museums worldwide, including the Metropolitan Museum of Art, the Smithsonian Institution, the Boston Museum of Fine Art, and Yad Vashem, the Holocaust memorial in Israel.

Goldberg was born in the shtetl of Kazimierz in central Poland. His village was famous throughout eastern Europe for composers of Hassidic music and generations of great rabbis. One of 11 children, he grew up living on the meager income of his shoemaker father. At the age of six, Chaim began sketching, using his father's shoe dyes as paint and his mother's folk songs as inspiration. Throughout his youth, he worked odd jobs after school to earn money for art supplies. When he was 14, a man visiting the shoe shop saw his work and helped him secure scholarships to attend art school in Krakow. By 17, he was accepted to the National Academy of Fine Arts in Warsaw, making him the youngest student to ever attend the school.

The artist's aspirations were stunted by World War II. Goldberg served in the Polish Army and was taken prisoner by the Germans. After fleeing the prison camp, he tried to rescue his family, but they refused to leave. Chaim left Poland with his bride-to-be, Rachel, her parents, and her sister. They spent weeks traveling a thousand rugged miles to Siberia in the U.S.S.R., where they endured the war years.

After the war, Goldberg traveled in a boxcar, along with thousands of other Polish refugees, back to Poland. He found the place he once called home in ruins and his family gone. Chaim stayed in Poland for five years and resumed his studies and work as an artist. He was commissioned by the Polish government to design a number of monuments, but his inspiration—his roots, his family, his people—was gone. "He could not create on a cemetery … The mass graves of millions of his beloved people were haunting him," wrote a fellow survivor who met the artist. Goldberg left Poland, moved to Israel, and finally settled in the United States in 1966. He and his wife raised two sons.

Goldberg continues creating works of art immortalizing the victims of the Holocaust and keeping alive the memory of so many murdered people and so many destroyed villages. Works such as *Trains, Prayer, Final Goodbye, Resistance, Message 1943,* and others make the suffering and the horror come alive and the voices of misery speak.

Nobel laureate and Yiddish writer Isaac Bashevis Singer says of this artist: "Goldberg came from the shtetl and remembers its every detail. He is never abstract but is true to the objects and their divine order. His work is enriching Jewish art and the image of our tradition. The shtetl of Chaim Goldberg reflects the despair and sadness of the past and delight and hope of our people for our future."

"If people will relate to each other, if we will dance together and be happy together, it will be a better world in which we live."

ANGIE & MORITZ GOLDFEIER

JEWELERS, PHILANTHROPISTS & HOLOCAUST SURVIVORS

They brought five beautiful grandchildren. God should watch over them and bless them all," wrote the Goldfeiers about their own two children, and their children's children. For survivors of the Holocaust, the children are the most precious testimony to their survival.

Angie and Moritz Goldfeier were nearly children themselves when they met after the war. He was 17 and she was 15. Moritz had been liberated from Auschwitz with his 14-year-old brother, Berek, on May 5, 1945. The brothers were the only surviving members of their family. By October of that year, they made their way westward to Regensburg, Germany. It was rumored that there they could get visas for Palestine.

"I wish we had never gone to that town," says Moritz, as he recalls the tragedy in Regensburg. Instead of getting a ticket to freedom, the Germans murdered his little brother Berek, killing him for a bit of money and his gold watch. "I was able to shelter him from harm for almost a year (after liberation) until this tragic end."

The brothers had endured the camps, the ghetto, and terror in their hometown of Brzeziny, Poland, as the war began in 1939. Moritz says, "I recall very vividly the summer of 1939 ... we were in the country during our vacation ... everybody was nervous and scared." Moritz's family returned home early from vacation that year and soon heard the news that the Germans had invaded Poland. The Germans ordered all men to assemble in front of their homes in the morning. They were taken away to work—some never returned home. These work selections continued for weeks. Next came the order that Jews had to wear armbands showing the Star of David.

More orders: Jews were not allowed to assemble in groups of more than three people. The Brzeziny Synagogue was burned to the ground and the rabbi murdered. "From that moment on, I do not remember going to the synagogue anymore."

Moritz's family, formerly in the clothing business, survived in the Brzeziny ghetto by manufacturing uniforms for the German Army. Even young Moritz worked as a tailor. As the darkness of war and persecution hung over them, Moritz's mother arranged for him to study for his Bar Mitzvah. He recited the blessings and his Haftorah in secrecy at the tailor shop, with a group of men as witnesses.

The terror continued. Moritz's two-year-old brother was taken from the family during a ghetto "selection." Soon the Brzeziny ghetto was liquidated. Moritz and his remaining two siblings and parents were moved to the ghetto of Lodz. Selections continued. At the end of 1944, the remaining Jews in Lodz were deported to Auschwitz. Moritz never saw his parents or sister again. He and his brother were selected for a work camp.

They were liberated by the Russians in 1945 and went to Germany. Moritz met Angie, the 15-year-old girl who later became his wife. It was she and other close friends who helped ease his sorrow when Berek was killed. The couple was married in 1948. They intended to immigrate to Israel, but when their visas arrived, they discovered they had accidentally registered to go to America.

"This was our destiny," recalls Moritz. They arrived in New York City on August 5, 1950. Angie was homesick, and at age 21, she was the mother of their one-year-old son. Moritz, 23, recognized a future for his family. He began importing antiques from Europe, then moved into the diamond and jewelry business. The Goldfeiers had a second child, and are now living their dream—enjoying a home overlooking Central Park and being with their five grandchildren.

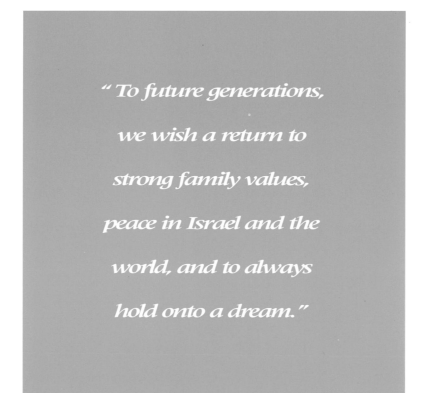

" To future generations, we wish a return to strong family values, peace in Israel and the world, and to always hold onto a dream."

JONA GOLDRICH

CONSTRUCTION COMPANY EXECUTIVE, PHILANTHROPIST & SURVIVOR OF THE TURKA GHETTO AND CHILD OF THE HOLOCAUST

There is not a day that goes by that I do not think about it," says Jona Goldrich. Of living in hiding, of secret travels in darkness, of the numerous escapes from the Nazis, and of the years he and his brother endured while they were just children, without their parents.

Goldrich was born in Turka, Poland. Nazis captured the town in 1941. Jona was 14 years old. The Nazis immediately instituted policies of forced labor, armband identification, and a prohibition against giving food to Jews. Many Jews starved to death in the Turka ghetto in the winter of 1941–1942. Then, the "aktions" began. These were efforts by the Nazis to create havoc and unrest among the Jews. They often included deportations, mass murders, or hangings.

Goldrich and his family survived the feared children's aktion, where thousands of little children were taken from their parents and murdered. Jona and his family also survived the "Great Aktion," the deportation of nearly all the remaining Jews to the camps. By the end of 1942, the town's Jewish population of 10,000 had been reduced to only a handful of people.

Goldrich's father had been a successful lumber businessman and was one of the most active members of the Turka Jewish community. Well versed in Talmudic studies, he was an active member of "Akiva," a Zionist group that encouraged people, especially young people, to make "Aliya" and move to Israel. His mother also was very active in charitable causes, serving children and the poor.

When the Gestapo began to conduct house-to-house searches, Jona, his parents, and his younger brother hid in the attic. His older brother ran into the mountains to hide. The family stayed in the attic for four days, waiting for the inevitable. Then, quietly huddled together in their tiny attic space, they listened as the Gestapo entered and searched their home. The Germans did not find the Goldrich family.

Goldrich learned that another "aktion" was planned—a "Judenfrei aktion" to make Turka "free of Jews." In an attempt to save their children, Goldrich's parents sent him and his younger brother to live with cousins in Hungary. Jona, only a teen himself, was now responsible for the welfare of his 12-year-old brother. Led by a hired guide, the young boys traveled at night through the heavily wooded mountains. When they arrived at the home of their cousins, Goldrich knew that Polish refugees would not be safe with this prominent family, so he found another place to live. Still not safe, the two boys went to Budapest.

Jona thought it was only a matter of time before the Germans would march into Hungary. On daily visits to the Palestine Office in Budapest, he begged, pleaded, and cajoled officials into allowing his brother and him to be part of a secret transport to Israel. Eventually, the officials relented. Posing as Hungarians, the brothers embarked on their dangerous passage to the Holy Land. En route, Goldrich learned that their passage had been bought from the Germans and that they could be betrayed anywhere along the way.

Jona Goldrich lived in Israel for 10 years. He fought in the 1948 War of Independence and was the only non-Sabra member of an elite commando unit. He later went to France to help Holocaust survivors find their way to Israel. In 1950, he came to New York as an engineer on an Israeli merchant ship. He finally settled in California where he and a partner began their own construction business. Goldrich's brother remained in Israel.

"In spite of adversity and incredible conditions, you can direct your destiny by relying on faith, luck, and your own persistence and courage."

HENNY GURKO

SINGER, SONGWRITER, POET & SURVIVOR OF THE VILNA GHETTO AND
KAISERWALD, STUTTHOF, AND DACHAU CONCENTRATION CAMPS

Her pillars of strength were her father, Akiva Durmashkin—a musician, conductor, composer, and impresario—and her brother Vladimir—child prodigy, composer, musical producer, director, and conductor. It is no wonder, then, that for Henny Durmashkin Gurko, music was her salvation.

"Our house was always filled with music. Music poured into the streets from the open windows of every room and could be heard blocks away. People said that in our house even the walls were musical!" Gurko's house was in Vilna, Poland. Her father composed liturgical and Hassidic music. He worked with the greatest cantors of Europe in the "Great Synagogue" of Vilna. Vladimir began appearing in his father's concerts at age six. By age 25, he was the conductor of the Philharmonic Orchestra in Vilna. Henny was to become a coloratura soprano.

Henny was scheduled to audition on the radio singing Mozart's "The Magic Flute" on September 1, 1939—the day World War II began. Vilna came under Soviet control. While conditions for the Jews worsened, Gurko continued her musical training, and she was accepted to sing in the Vilna City Choir—the only Jew.

By the summer of 1941, German soldiers moved into Vilna. The Gestapo made house-to-house raids searching for young Jewish men to be used as laborers, many of whom never returned. With only 15 minutes' notice, the family was herded into the Vilna ghetto, along with 50,000 other Jews. Thousands of Jews were sent to the camps and thousands more were taken to Ponary just outside Vilna. Ponary was a wooded area surrounded by heavy barbed wire. Jews were brought there under heavy guard, stripped and robbed of their valuables, and shot. That is how Henny's father died.

Vladimir, meanwhile, was the stimulus for an active cultural life in the ghetto. In 1941, he formed a Hebrew choir and orchestra, of which Gurko was a part. Smuggling a piano, music, and instruments into the ghetto, more than 100 musicians joined together to offer ghetto concerts. Vladimir also continued to compose music, including an orchestral piece entitled "The Eulogy of Ponary."

In 1943, the Vilna ghetto was liquidated. Vladimir was sent to Klooga, a labor camp in Estonia. Henny's mother was among those "selected" for death in the gas chambers. Gurko was put on a cattle car and sent to the concentration camps—first Kaiserwald near Riga, Latvia, then to another labor camp. From there, she was sent to Stutthof, then to a labor camp in Lithuania, and later to Landsberg, part of the Dachau complex.

Even in the camps, music was a part of Gurko's life. She would sing to her fellow prisoners in the barrack, and the SS guards, once they heard her lilting voice, ordered her to sing. She performed regular concerts for the camp inmates. "I will never forget the audiences—my dear, poor sisters and brothers in sorrow, my sad audiences … I always tried to give them my best, although it was always hard facing them from the stage." On May 1, 1945, the nightmare ended as Americans liberated Dachau. Vladimir was not as lucky. Just one hour before he was to have been liberated from Klooga, the Nazis shot all the inmates.

Following liberation, Gurko performed for survivors and refugees in DP camps. With growing popularity, she and an orchestra played throughout Europe. In 1948, Leonard Bernstein joined the orchestra to perform in two displacement camps and also in Munich.

Henny Gurko met her future husband on the boat that carried her to the United States in 1950. They married, raised three children, and Gurko continued her singing. She recorded an album of ghetto songs titled "Songs to Remember." One song, "A Life of Pain," includes these lyrics:

> *"Let go of your sorrow, there is always tomorrow … and after the rain, the sun will shine again!"*

SIEGFRIED HALBREICH

AUTHOR, RETIRED PHARMACIST, BUSINESSMAN & SURVIVOR OF SACHSENHAUSEN, GROSS-ROSEN, AUSCHWITZ-BUNA, AND NORDHAUSEN-DORA CONCENTRATION CAMPS

For Auschwitz No. 68233, survival meant five and a half torturous years in four, horror-filled camps. His 2,000 days of imprisonment meant close to 50,000 hours of struggle to keep himself alive. The number that mattered the most, however, was the number of lives of his fellow Jews and Gentiles he was able to save.

Siegfried Halbreich was born in the southern Polish town of Dziedzice in 1909. In 1929, he began working as a pharmaceutical apprentice in Germany. He had served as a reserve officer in the Polish Army and later studied at the University of Krakow to become a pharmacist. While trying to escape from German-occupied Poland to Yugoslavia, he was turned over to the Gestapo by a German spy in the Yugoslav Army. He was deported to Sachsenhausen concentration camp. That was in 1939.

In 1941, Halbreich was sent to Gross-Rosen for a year, then to Auschwitz for over two years, and later to the Nordhausen-Dora camp. He spent from 1939 to 1945 in the camps, desperately struggling to stay alive. "Living in the camps, we had to stifle our urge to kill the Germans. Nothing would come from it but our own death and that of others. When we had time to think about our situation, it became clear that the best way to retaliate against the Germans was to live and to keep as many people alive as we could," wrote Halbreich in his memoirs, *Before—During—After.*

Siegfried's work in the camps varied, from hauling rock to sorting medications when they arrived at an SS hospital. Because of his pharmaceutical training, he later was assigned to work in a camp hospital at Auschwitz-Buna where he had more protection from the elements than most other prisoners. He also had a chance to save others from death. "I

"Through strength and conviction, all is never lost."

continued my work against the Germans. The more of us who remained alive, the more difficult it was for the Germans. I admitted younger prisoners into the hospital when there weren't enough beds, crossed people off the transport lists, and hid young prisoners during selections by transferring them from one room to another."

Halbreich was liberated by the Americans in Nordhausen in April 1945. "I believe that one of the reasons for my success was that I had courage and acted on my own. I did what seemed best at the moment, and, I wasn't caught," he said.

Because he spoke some English, Halbreich worked as an interpreter and investigator for the Americans in their war crimes investigations for the Nuremberg trials. He later became a member of the Board of Buna-Auschwitz Committee and was called many times to testify as a witness in the trials of the Nazi criminals. He also testified in 1960 in Jerusalem against Adolf Eichmann, the chief administrator of the Nazi "Final Solution."

Siegfried Halbreich immigrated to the United States in June 1946 and settled in Cleveland, Ohio. He later moved to California. He and his wife, Ruth, who is also a survivor, have two children and two grandchildren. Halbreich continues his efforts to save the history of those lives that were lost at Nazi hands. He remains active in a variety of organizations that deal with the Holocaust and combat anti-Semitism. He travels the world speaking to students and community groups about his concentration camp experiences, and estimates he has told his story more than 900 times. "When I lecture to students, my intention is not to re-create the horror that we lived through, but to help them to learn the warning signals of discrimination, prejudice, and injustice."

ROMAN I. HARTE

FILM PRODUCER, DIRECTOR, MEMBER OF THE
AMERICAN FILM INSTITUTE & SURVIVOR OF THE RZESZOW GHETTO

Roman Harte was just a youngster when he held his first camera. Fascinated with images, his camera became his constant companion as he captured moments and memories on film. Today, memories are all Harte has left of his immediate family of six—all were killed in the Holocaust.

Harte, born Abraham Hersh Heinberg, was raised with his three older sisters in the town of Rzeszow in southern Poland. His father was a livestock broker and his mother was a bookkeeper. Both worked hard to have Harte educated in a private Polish school.

One of his sisters moved to Israel in 1937. In 1940, at the age of 16, Roman was sent by the Nazis from his hometown to a labor camp where he and other prisoners worked building a dam. Later, the camp was liquidated, and most of the inmates were sent to Auschwitz, but not Roman. Harte managed to escape and returned home to his family.

Home was now the Rzeszow ghetto, where the town's large Jewish population was living. Harte became part of a Jewish underground organization and acted as a liaison for the Polish home army. His compatriots helped Roman obtain false documents, identifying him as a non-Jew. He remained in the ghetto until 1943 when the Nazis liquidated the ghetto. His immediate family was murdered in the Belzec death camp in the southeastern part of Poland.

Meanwhile, Harte's falsified documents enabled him to travel to Austria and find work as a farm laborer near the town of Zell am See. There he remained until 1945, when he was arrested by the Nazis for political activities, and sentenced to a Gestapo prison in Innsbruck, Austria. Roman spent three months in prison until the American army liberated him. "After the war's end, I returned to Poland in search of any of my remaining family. I found no one alive."

Harte resumed his studies and graduated from the Polish Film Academy with a degree of Master of Fine Arts, specializing in motion picture film production. Harte became an accomplished film producer and worked with some of the most talented and world-renowned film directors of that time, including Jan Kadar, Roman Polanski, and Andrzej Vajda. Harte, too, was recognized internationally and has received numerous awards for his work in the motion picture industry.

But hatred and anti-Semitism continued to be pervasive forces in Poland. Because of that, Roman Harte immigrated to America with his wife and two children in 1968. For more than 20 years, Harte served as director of film production at the prestigious American Film Institute.

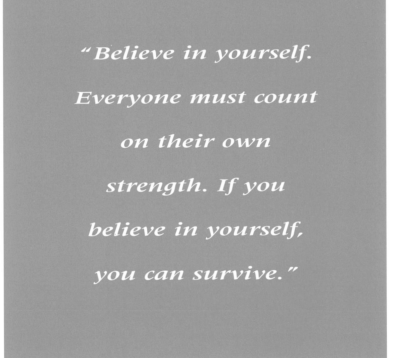

"Believe in yourself. Everyone must count on their own strength. If you believe in yourself, you can survive."

67

EVA & EMIL HECHT

EVA: HOLOCAUST SPEAKER & SURVIVOR OF AUSCHWITZ, LANDSBERG, AND DACHAU CONCENTRATION CAMPS
EMIL: RETIRED BUSINESS EXECUTIVE, HOLOCAUST SPEAKER & SURVIVOR OF AUSCHWITZ,
MAUTHAUSEN, GUSEN, AND GUNSKIRCHEN CONCENTRATION CAMPS

They had both been warned that their only way out of the concentration camps was through the smokestack of the crematorium. Today, Eva and Emil Hecht are survivors of the Holocaust and they speak freely and often about the dangers of hatred and intolerance. Eva is from Hungary and Emil was born in Czechoslovakia.

Eva was 16 years old when she entered Auschwitz. She and her sister, Magda, were separated from the rest of the family in the selection lines. Eva never forgot her father's parting words: "Watch out for Magda." Eva and her sister were together as they survived the Nazi concentration camps. Today, they live two blocks apart.

Also, today, Eva's memories are inescapable. She remembers Alice, a red-haired, 20-year-old Slovakian girl who was placed in charge of the 1,200 female inmates in Auschwitz's Barrack #9. Alice warned the inmates about being "fooled" by Dr. Josef Mengele, chief physician at Auschwitz, known as the Nazi "Angel of Death."

Mengele would enter the barracks, impeccably outfitted with white gloves, mirror-polished boots, and a crisply pressed SS uniform. A sweet and innocent-sounding Mengele would request all the ill and infirm in need of special treatment to step forward. He asked for any pregnant women to come, too, and assured them in a kind and gentle manner that their needs would be met. Anyone who stepped forward was sent to the gas chamber that night.

Young Alice, already a three-year veteran of the camp, had given the girls stern warnings against falling for Mengele's entrapment. So angered was she when his deception succeeded that she beat the few women who dared step forward. "To you, nothing matters anymore. Tonight, you will escape through the chimney!" Her cruelty was her way to instill a lifesaving message in the numbed psyche of the remaining inmates. "Each day you survive this hell," Alice said scornfully, "you are one day closer to freedom." In 1944, Eva was sent from Auschwitz to Landsberg, and then to Dachau. On April 29, 1945, she was liberated, along with her sister, Magda, by the Americans.

Emil also had been an inmate at Auschwitz. From there, he was sent to Mauthausen. Once there, prisoners selected for slave labor were made to stand at attention for hours. "Then an SS officer arrived with a whip and a German shepherd at his side. He pointed his whip at the tall chimney nearby and yelled, 'Jews, you see that over there? That is the only way out of here for you, through that chimney.'"

Next, Emil was sent to a labor camp called Gusen I. Though beaten and deprived of food and sleep, he helped drill tunnels into the mountain where Germans planned to shield their new airplane factories from Allied bombs.

Emil was 19 when he was standing at the end of a line of sick prisoners in the hospital at Gusen II; each was given an armpit thermometer to record their body temperature. A doctor was separating ill prisoners from the healthier inmates. Emil realized that a high temperature was a death sentence. Knowing he was ill, he held the thermometer between his two fingers in his armpit area, deftly exposing the instrument to the heat of his feverish skin for only the last moment. Emil produced a normal temperature reading. He was not among those sent to the gas chambers that day.

Near war's end, the crematorium being built to murder Emil and 17,000 other Jews was luckily not completed. Emil escaped death when General Patton's 3rd Army and the 761st African-American Tank Brigade liberated the prisoners at Günskirchen. He weighed only 66 pounds.

Eva and Emil Hecht met in 1947, and immigrated to the United States in 1951. They raised two children. They continue to educate youth in the community about the Holocaust.

"Spread knowledge, enlightenment, and tolerance among your fellowman."

FANYA HELLER

AUTHOR, HUMANITARIAN, PHILANTHROPIST, COMMUNITY ACTIVIST & HOLOCAUST SURVIVOR

Fanya Gottesfeld Heller says, "We are the last generation to give firsthand testimony about the Shoah. When we are gone, the world will have nothing more than the written record we have left behind." Now, Heller eagerly speaks out about the Holocaust, something that was not always possible for her to do.

Heller was born in the Polish shtetl Skala, later absorbed into the Ukraine as a result of the Hitler-Stalin Pact of 1939. When the Germans invaded Russia in 1941, Skala came under Nazi occupation and its Jewish residents were rounded up. When it became clear that the Nazis were determined to eliminate the entire Jewish population of the Ukraine, the Gottesfeld family decided that the only way to survive was to hide.

First, they hid in a cave under the workroom floor of an egg-exporting firm. Fanya's father, an engineer by profession, worked at night for weeks digging the cave in this warehouse located on the family property. Heller's family of 18 people, including her parents, younger brother, aunts, uncles, and cousins, all crammed into the cave in the predawn hours of September 26, 1942. That was when the Gestapo and the Ukrainian militia marched into town to kill the Jews of Skala. "I don't know how long it was until we heard footsteps above us, the unmistakable tread of heavy boots . . ." The Germans searched the warehouse, but did not discover the family.

As the war raged on, the family continued to hide. Fanya's charm and girlish beauty attracted the attention of Jan, a Ukrainian shoemaker turned militiaman. Under Nazi occupation, the man became a trusted friend of the family. He brought them bits of food and other supplies. For weeks, he hid Heller and her brother in the attic of his barn. Finally, he helped the family obtain shelter in the cramped attic of a Polish peasant. There they remained for two years.

" In working to strengthen the foundations of our people, we honor God's gift of life."

Throughout these months, Jan was a constant visitor. In time, touched by his devotion and self-sacrifice, Heller reciprocated Jan's love. Although Jan hoped that they would marry, Fanya knew that, despite her feelings for him, there was no way she could betray her father and her family by marrying out of her faith. Soon after the Russians liberated the area in 1944, Fanya's father vanished.

Heller and her remaining family left Skala in August 1945. She met her late husband, Joseph Heller, in Silesia, and they were married after a three-week courtship in Budapest. They moved to the United States in 1960 and operated a business together in New York City.

It was not until many, many years later that Fanya Heller began to share her memories and her feelings. In the 1980s, Heller began writing her memoirs, which were published in 1993 in a candid and vivid story of her experiences titled *Strange and Unexpected Love: A Teenage Girl's Holocaust Memoirs.*

"I had a responsibility to my children and grandchildren to open up and tell what happened to me," she said. Today, Fanya Heller shares her life with her three children, two daughters and one son, and eight grandchildren, and also with friends and the Jewish community. She is a frequent public speaker about the Holocaust and is a lifelong activist for Jewish causes. She serves on several boards and is a benefactor and a recipient of an honorary Doctor of Humane Letters from Yeshiva University.

Fanya Heller shares this thought on renewal and the future: The Ba'al Shem Tov, the eighteenth-century Hassidic master tells us, "God's gift to mankind is a world that is new to us every morning, and a person shall believe that he is reborn each day."

RYSZARD HOROWITZ

INTERNATIONAL AWARD-WINNING PHOTO COMPOSER & SURVIVOR OF AUSCHWITZ
AND THE YOUNGEST MEMBER OF SCHINDLER'S LIST

Behind the extraordinary images of renowned photographer Ryszard Horowitz is an even more extraordinary story of survival.

Horowitz was four months old when the German Army invaded Poland in 1939. His infancy and toddlerhood were spent in the ghetto of Krakow. In 1943, Ryszard and a cousin were secretly sent to the countryside to live with an uncle to avoid death in the liquidation of the Krakow ghetto. His parents were deported to the Plaszow forced-labor camp.

Ryszard's father, who was working in the camp in charge of supplies, learned that the area where his son was hiding was soon to be liquidated. He managed to sneak then four-year-old Horowitz and his cousin into the camp to save them. His father then arranged for his wife, daughter, and Ryszard to work in the factory of Oskar Schindler. It was this factory owner whose story is told in the 1993 Oscar-winning Steven Spielberg film, *Schindler's List.* Horowitz was the youngest person to be saved by Schindler.

Schindler's factory was shut down in the spring of 1944. Horowitz and his family went back to Plaszow. In May of that year, 1,400 "unproductive" adults and 286 children were loaded on freight cars and sent to Auschwitz-Birkenau to be gassed. Horowitz survived with nine other children by hiding in the barracks of the Jewish police at the Plaszow camp. Soon, Schindler opened another factory in Brünnlitz, Czechoslovakia, where Horowitz, four other boys, and 800 men were destined to work. On the way to the factory, their train was diverted to the Gross-Rosen concentration camp. Somehow the boys evaded the guards for three days until the train was allowed to continue to Schindler's new factory.

Soon, however, every child in the factory was rounded up. Ryszard and his father, along with all the children, were sent to Auschwitz. Once there, he was separated from his father who was forced to march to Mauthausen labor camp. Horowitz survived in Auschwitz for several months. One day, he was in a line of children about to be shot by Nazi guards. Suddenly, a German officer arrived on a motorcycle and reported on the imminent approach of the Red Army. The Germans abandoned the camp. Horowitz is one of the youngest known survivors of Auschwitz.

Ryszard was taken to an orphanage in Krakow where he was adopted by a family friend. The same family also adopted Roman Polanski, now an internationally known filmmaker. Horowitz's mother assumed her son was dead, but discovered he was alive when she recognized him in a Russian Army film documenting the liberation of Auschwitz.

Miraculously, most of his immediate family survived the camps and they reestablished their lives in Krakow. There, Horowitz studied fine arts and majored in painting. While he was still in his late teens, Krakow emerged as the center of avant-garde painting, theater production, and filmmaking. It was during that time that Horowitz became fascinated with American photography.

In 1959, Ryszard came to the United States after having secured a scholarship to study at Pratt Institute. He studied with famed photographer and designer Alexey Brodovitch. Since 1967, Horowitz has operated his own studio, from which have flowed creative masterpieces that are collected, exhibited, and published worldwide.

Horowitz has pioneered the use of traditional photography and computer technology to create photo-realistic compositions. His works are frequently whimsical; some depict humor and others are theatrical. All are strikingly colorful and extraordinarily imaginative. With understatement, Horowitz says, "That's the way I am, and fortunately for me I managed to transform my tragic childhood experience into something that is extremely optimistic and positive." Today, he works and lives with his wife and two sons in Manhattan.

"Life is what is important."

CLARA ISAACMAN

AUTHOR, EDUCATOR, LECTURER & MEMBER OF THE BELGIAN UNDERGROUND, AND HOLOCAUST SURVIVOR

She did not see sunlight or breathe fresh air for two and one half years. Clara Isaacman hid with her family in 18 different places between the summer of 1942 and the spring of 1945—sometimes in rat-infested cellars, sometimes in homes—always, always in darkness.

Isaacman, born Clara Heller in Romania, moved with her family to Antwerp, Belgium, to escape the rising tide of anti-Semitism. There they lived a normal life of a middle-class family until 1942. They were reluctant to leave this home during the war; Clara's father did not believe Hitler intended to kill the Jews. Isaacman remembers the event that convinced them otherwise.

"One afternoon, without telling my family, I skipped Hebrew school to go to a birthday party. When I got home from the party, our house was in an uproar. Mama was crying. Daddy was pacing the floor. Neighbors were sobbing, clinging to one another. When Mama noticed me standing in the doorway staring at them in bewilderment, she gave a shriek and rushed toward me. 'Clara, Clara,' was all she and Daddy could say as they embraced me. Little by little, everyone told me his or her version of what happened that afternoon. A German army truck had been parked across the entrance to my Hebrew school. All of the teachers and children inside the school were herded into the truck and driven away. I didn't question the quirk of fate that had kept me away. I could only think, I should have been there. Where were my friends now? Where were they going? Would the teachers look after them? How would I have behaved had I been with them? The incident at my Hebrew school showed us the true face of the beast that was bearing down on us. But it was too late. Every known avenue of escape had been closed. We were trapped."

"Everything you do is important because you are exchanging a day of your life for it. Make it count for something purposeful."

The family went into hiding. "There were times when I dared not move. All I could do was just sit there for hours. And every time I heard a noise or a footstep, I thought it was the Gestapo or SS coming to kill me."

One night, Clara's father ventured to the home of people he believed to be sympathetic to the Jews. He brought them diamonds and jewels to trade for bread. He was betrayed by those people and was later gassed to death while he was asleep in his apartment in Antwerp. Her older brother also was killed at Auschwitz.

Fifty thousand Jews lived in Antwerp before the war. When Isaacman was liberated in April of 1945, she was one of the 5,000 who survived. For her efforts with the Belgian underground, Isaacman received a treasured citation from King Leopold III.

After the German defeat, Clara met a young American soldier named Danny who had come to a community center to offer his help to the remaining Jews of Antwerp. They married, came to the United States, completed their education, and embarked on long careers of teaching and service to the international community. When he died in 1982, Dr. Daniel Isaacman was president of Gratz College.

Today, Clara Isaacman is a survivor delivering history with a voice of passion. She has written her memoirs in a moving book titled *Clara's Story*. She has also written a manual for teachers about teaching the Holocaust to young people. It took nearly 50 years after the Holocaust for Isaacman to write her book—50 years for the pain to recede enough for her to talk about what happened. In her writings and in her classroom lectures, Isaacman warns audiences that man's inhumanity will kill us again and again if we continue to dismiss history as irrelevant to everyone today.

ANN & ED KAYE

ANN: SURVIVOR OF THE BEREZA AND PRUZANA GHETTOS, AND AUSCHWITZ CONCENTRATION CAMP
ED: COMMUNITY VOLUNTEER & SURVIVOR OF THE PRUZANA GHETTO AND FREEDOM FIGHTER

After the endless beatings and brutal killings of the Holocaust, seeing a friendly face was like a gift from heaven. Ann Pomeraniec (now Ann Kaye) recalls seeing Mendel Kaganowicz (now known as Ed Kaye): "I almost collapsed with happiness to see someone who knew me before Auschwitz," Ann says of the reunion with Ed in 1946.

Ann was only 16 when the Nazis forced Jews in her hometown of Bereza Kartuska into the ghetto. In less than a year, that ghetto was liquidated. Nazis took the Jews to a forested area where mass murders occurred after the victims dug their own graves. Ann survived only because her father had built a hideout in one of the walls of their house. The family hid and escaped to another ghetto. Now 17, Ann escaped one more time to the Pruzana ghetto 35 kilometers away on the northeastern border of Poland. There she met Ed in 1942. In 1943, they parted. Ed escaped and joined a partisan group. Ann was deported to Auschwitz.

"The dirt and filth of Auschwitz are impossible to describe. I was shaved and put in a dress and a pair of clogs. It was winter and people were dying. I had to step over dead bodies. If I didn't go to work, I felt I would die, too."

While imprisoned, Ann suffered typhoid, pleurisy, dysentery, and malaria on three separate occasions. One day, stricken with a high fever, she did not report to work. "Those who could not work were required to sit outside the barrack, and a truck would come by to take you to the crematorium. I was waiting with two other girls when the vehicle arrived and I was helped onto the truck."

"The driver told us, 'Don't worry, they are not going to gas you today.' I thought he was lying. But 15 minutes outside of Auschwitz, I could see that he was not heading toward the gas chamber, but into another camp area. In a clandestine maneuver, the Nazis had filled one barrack with sick girls to assure the Red Cross inspectors that we were being properly cared for ... I was delirious at the time and was unaware that the Red Cross inspection never occurred. My life was spared when the head nurse hid me under a pile of rags and blankets. The remaining sick prisoners were taken away and their fate is unknown." Ann was liberated in 1945.

While Ann was in Auschwitz, Ed had escaped to the woods in an attempt to join the partisans. He was instrumental in disrupting the flow of Nazi troops and military material to and from the front by destroying railroad tracks, trains, and bridges. He was wounded three times. Shot in the leg during an attack on a German garrison, Ed was left behind in the forest so as not to slow the other partisans' escape. They left Ed with his handgun so that if he were captured, he could shoot himself. Twelve hours later, a friend returned and took Ed to a hospital. There were no doctors and no medicine. He returned to his partisan mission in six weeks.

After years of near-death experiences, Ed and Ann were reunited in February of 1946. They married shortly after that and immigrated to the United States in 1949. Since the war, the Kayes have spoken to countless audiences about the horrors of the Holocaust. Ed also volunteers at a food bank for the needy.

> "Teach the young to love, not hate ... every human being deserves to live, no matter the religion or the race."

ROMAN KENT

BUSINESS EXECUTIVE, COMMUNITY ACTIVIST & SURVIVOR OF THE LODZ GHETTO AND AUSCHWITZ, GROSS-ROSEN, AND FLOSSENBÜRG CONCENTRATION CAMPS

I didn't care what the date was. All I cared about was how I could make it through the day," said Roman Kent. "I don't know exactly when it was I was rounded up in the Lodz ghetto and sent to Auschwitz. I don't know how many days I traveled in the cattle car without food, without water. Time was meaningless."

What Kent does remember is that from the start of World War II to the end, he was trapped in the ghetto, herded into a concentration camp, moved from one camp to another, and was starved and beaten. He was interned at Auschwitz, Gross-Rosen, and finally Flossenbürg.

Roman was a teenager during the war. "Winter was coming when I was in Gross-Rosen with 805 other youths. We heard rumors that we were going to be sent back to Auschwitz to the crematorium. The rumors persisted in spite of the fact that they sent us to work daily. One day when they rounded us up in the square and counted us as they normally did, two children were missing. After searching for them for several hours, the SS dogs found the missing children.

"I overheard the camp commandant remark to his subordinate, 'They had so much guts to hide themselves, let them stay.' I expected the two to be killed on the spot for their escape attempt. Realizing the importance of the commandant's remarks, I suddenly jumped out of line and told the commandant that I was there with my brother, and we were both young and strong, and we would like to stay there and work. That incident alone could have ended my life. Instead, my brother and I were given permission to stay. The remaining 800 were returned to Auschwitz and gassed."

"Participate in life, set goals, and try to achieve them. Don't be a bystander; be involved and get involved."

Kent and his brother were liberated by the U.S. Army in 1945. The two immigrated to the United States and attended Emory University in Atlanta. His brother went on to become a very accomplished neurosurgeon on the West Coast, but died while still a young man. Today, Kent continues to operate a successful import business that he started after college.

For Roman Kent, however, monetary gains pale when measured against personal, philanthropic, and humanitarian accomplishments. To that end, Kent produced a documentary about the 1.5 million Jewish children killed in the Holocaust. *Children of the Holocaust* received critical acclaim and was shown several times on national television in 1980. "This is something that I wanted to leave for my children and other children." Kent describes the end of the movie where the narrator says, "At the beginning, there were children. At the end, for one and a half million children, only ashes. For the few survivors, memories. No answers, no meaning, only memories and questions. Where was God, where was man, where were you and I, and for all of us, the ultimate question: Where will we be next time when children cry out in pain?"

Today, Roman actively participates in a number of organizations that fight hatred and that are dedicated to preserving the history of the Holocaust, including the Jewish Foundation for Christian Rescuers, the American Gathering of Jewish Holocaust Survivors, the Anti-Defamation League, and others.

"The triumph is that somehow, I and other survivors, in spite of what we went through, were able to put ourselves together, and had the guts and the audacity to start from the beginning and create a new life."

KRISTINE KEREN, D.D.S.

DENTIST, MOTHER & SURVIVOR OF THE SEWERS OF LVOV, POLAND

There was only one place left to hide. As the Nazis were about to liquidate the ghetto of Lvov, Kristine Keren's father dug a hole through the floor and into the sewers of the city. There they stayed, without a glimmer of sunshine, for 14 months.

Keren, then Kristine Chiger, was six when the Germans invaded her Polish town in 1941. To escape the Germans, Kristine, her younger brother, Pawel, and her parents fled from one place to another, always staying one step ahead of the Nazis. The family was forced into the ghetto and her parents both worked in labor camps. That meant that Kristine was responsible for the care of her three-year-old brother. "I got so sensitive that I could recognize German footsteps and I knew when to hide."

Fearful for their lives, the two found hiding places in suitcases, under beds, behind curtains, and under an artificial floor beneath a window. Cramped in the small spaces for hours at a time, the frightened youngsters learned to restrain their tears. "Even though he was so little, he never cried," Kristine said of her baby brother.

These hiding places were but a preparation for a more sinister sanctuary that saved Keren and her family. In 1943, when the Germans were liquidating the ghetto, Kristine's father gave everything he owned to a Christian sewer worker, Leopold Socha. With his help, Kristine and her family of four, along with six others, survived the Holocaust by hiding in the sewage-filled and rat-infested city sewers from 1943 to 1944.

"Mr. Socha brought us food very faithfully. But there were dangers. A few times, somebody found us, and we had to run through the tunnels. And once there was a heavy rainstorm, and the water was almost to the ceiling, which was less than five feet high. My parents, who were constantly bent, held us children up above the water so we could breathe.

"We never went outside or saw daylight, and it was dark, with webs all over and moss hanging on the wall. We slept on boards, and we had a small lamp, but that was it. You might think we were afraid of the rats. They were all over us but we got used to them, we played with them. But my father had to stay up at night so he could chase the rats away from eating our bread.

"Nobody had to tell us to be quiet. I felt like an animal. I went by instinct. But I became very, very depressed, and I didn't want to eat or to talk to anybody. That was when Leopold Socha picked me up and took me through the tunnels and said, 'Look up,' and I saw the daylight, and he said to me, 'You have to be very strong and one day you will go up there and live a life like other children.' My mother was always saying that Socha was an angel that God sent to save us."

> *"Even during the darkest moments of history, courage and dignity can withstand the greatest evil, and the will to survive can result in the triumph of the human spirit."*

Freedom came when the Russians arrived in July 1944. Emerging from the manhole, Kristine was blinded by the light. Her sight returned, and for Keren, nine years old by then, childhood could begin at last.

The family went to Krakow and later moved to Israel. In 1968, Kristine immigrated to the United States. She is now a dentist in New York and has a family of her own. Her mother lives in Israel. Her father, whom she calls a very brave man, passed away in 1975. Her brother also died, at the age of 39, while performing active military service with the Israeli Army.

ARNOLD KLEIN

RETIRED SALES REPRESENTATIVE & SURVIVOR OF AUSCHWITZ, BUCHENWALD, AND MAGDEBURG CONCENTRATION CAMPS

"To survive, you have to have a strong will. For some reason, I knew I was going to make it," says Arnold Klein.

Klein was born in Alesd, Romania. He and his parents lived in their hometown until 1944. But by 1941, that part of Romania had been ceded to Hungary.

"We helped the few Polish Jews who came through to escape, but we didn't believe it would happen to us. Anti-Semitism had been there all the time, but it was getting worse and worse." In 1944, Adolf Eichmann was sent to Hungary to liquidate the Jews and Klein and his parents were transported to Auschwitz.

As Klein tells the story, he was in a selection line at Auschwitz when he was confronted by the Nazi known as the Angel of Death, Josef Mengele. Mengele asked Klein how old he was. "I don't know why, but in my high school German, I told Mengele I was 18 instead of 16, and that saved my life." Klein was ordered to go to the left with his father, instead of to the right where thousands of Jews went to the gas chambers. Arnold and his father were assigned to Auschwitz's Camp A. Ten days later they were sent to Buchenwald.

In the early summer of 1944, Klein was separated from his father and was sent on a work transport to Magdeburg. The group included 2,864 prisoners, and they worked in a factory that made fuel from coal for the war effort. The factory was destroyed by American bombs and in January 1945 the prisoners were sent back to Buchenwald. By then, only 600 of the prisoners remained alive. They traveled for four days without food or water. Upon arrival at the camp, only 300 prisoners were still living. They were sent to take showers and were forced to wait in line naked, in subzero temperatures. Many died before reaching the showers. "It was complete hell."

By the time the camp was liberated in the spring of that year, only 71 prisoners from the original work transport of 2,864 were still alive. American tanks rolled into the camp on the afternoon of April 11, 1945. Klein's 6' 1" body had been reduced to 60 pounds.

"My memory of seeing the Angel of Death—of seeing Mengele's face—is a blur to me," explains Klein. "But one face I vividly remember is the face of a professional man, most likely an engineer in Magdeburg. Both he and I witnessed a German shepherd dog dragging the body of a Jew down the street. He knew what was happening to us and he was horrified, but he turned away. He could not bear to watch. He could not bear to see the atrocity that, through his silence, he helped to condone."

After liberation, Klein, along with 500 other surviving youngsters, was taken to France by the American Red Cross. He waited in Paris for a visa to the United States. He knew he had relatives there and he also now knew that both his parents had perished in the camps.

Arnold Klein immigrated to New York in 1948 and there he was diagnosed with tuberculosis. He was sent to Denver, Colorado, for treatment at the city's TB sanitarium. In Denver, Klein worked as a businessman and retail salesman. He also worked in restaurant management and in social services. Additionally, he worked as a fundraiser for the National Jewish Hospital in Denver.

Klein has a daughter and a son. He speaks frequently to schools and community groups about his experiences.

> *"Complacency is more dangerous than hatred. Be aware of what is happening around you, and do something about it."*

FRED KORT

ENTREPRENEUR, INTERNATIONAL BUSINESS EXECUTIVE, TOY MAKER,
PHILANTHROPIST & SURVIVOR OF GHETTOS AND LABOR AND DEATH CAMPS

Fred Kort likens his survival of the Holocaust to luck in a field of land mines.

"Picture a road," he says, "5,000 miles long and 6 feet wide. Each thousand miles represents one year of my life in the ghettos and camps. The road is planted with underground mines, each laid a foot and a half apart. I walked that 5,000-mile road and, whatever the reasons, I never stepped on a mine. It might have been because of youth, health, luck, courage, circumstances, hope, and, of course, faith."

Born in Germany, Kort survived five years in Nazi ghettos and concentration camps. He is one of only nine people in the world to have survived the Treblinka death camp in eastern Poland. Kort and his family lived in both Vienna and southern Germany before his family was deported to Poland in 1938. Once the war broke out a year later, through circumstances, the Kort family was separated. His mother and sister found themselves in Russian territory. His father was in Warsaw, while young Fred and his brother were forced into the Lodz ghetto. From there, he escaped and subsequently ended up first in the Warsaw ghetto, and later in several Nazi labor camps. The last labor camp was liquidated in July 1943, and all 2,000 prisoners were transferred to Treblinka. Treblinka was not a concentration camp, but was a death factory where more than 1 million people were murdered in little more than a year.

During the selection process, Kort was assigned to the labor detail in the camp. He survived bullets and beatings from the SS officers and guards. From the day of his arrival, it appeared that Fred would end up in the gas chambers. One day, he narrowly escaped that fate when an SS officer suddenly changed his mind and directed Kort to join a group of workers. In July 1944, the Russian Front was advancing. The German soldiers stormed the inner camp and began liquidating the remaining prisoners. In the commotion, Kort escaped to a storage shed, and hid by piling wood over himself. There he lay quietly late into the night. Then, in the darkness, he used his hands to dig under the camp's barbed-wire fences and escaped into the forest. Soldiers spotted him and began shooting, but without success.

After three weeks in the forest, he joined the Polish underground and he was later inducted into the Polish Army. He was 18. The war ended the following year, and Fred was reunited with his mother and sister, who had survived the war years deep inside Russia. Kort's father, brother, and more than 60 close family members perished in the Holocaust.

Kort came to the United States in 1947. He worked at various jobs while attending night school to learn the English language. Due to some knowledge of the electrical field, he was able to land a position as an assistant electrician at the Los Angeles Biltmore Hotel. One day, a hotel guest approached young Fred and asked if he knew anyone who could help him set up a toy factory. Kort said he did know someone—himself.

Kort joined Fesco Enterprises, which became the first company on the West Coast to manufacture bottled bubble toys. In 1969, Fred created his own company, the Imperial Toy Corporation. Today, Imperial's product line includes more than 800 items and reaches more than 50 foreign markets with factories in five countries.

Fred Kort and his family support numerous children's charities through donations of both toys and funds. He is one of the original founders of the U.S. Holocaust Memorial Museum. The Korts also donate to charities benefiting the State of Israel, and to other good causes around the world. In a national television program, Kort was dubbed a modern Jewish hero, along with Golda Meir, Albert Einstein, violinist Itzhak Perlman, and baseball player Hank Greenberg.

" Liberty and freedom are the greatest gifts a child can have. Appreciate the opportunities and complain less."

RAE KUSHNER

BUSINESS EXECUTIVE, PHILANTHROPIST & SURVIVOR OF THE NOVOGRUDEK GHETTO

On Shabbat, the German planes came and the bombs started to fall. The war against Russia had started and the city was on fire. Everyone started to run away from the town. We were listening to the radio. The bombs stopped and an announcement came over the radio that all the Jews should come back to town. The Germans told us, 'Don't be afraid. You're going to be safe and we will be good to you.'"

That was how Rae Kushner's nightmare began in 1941. She and her family lived in the northern Polish city of Novogrudek. The population was 25,000, 6,000 of them Jews. While anti-Semitism existed before the war, no one in Kushner's family could imagine what would happen to them over the next four years. "People told us, 'They [the Germans] are killing Jews.' We didn't believe them. We said, 'What kind of people would do that?'"

A month after the Germans ordered all the Jews back to the town, Kushner and her family were forced into a ghetto. The 6,000 Jews of Novogrudek were joined by another 24,000 Jews from surrounding small towns, and then the horrors began.

One Saturday, the Germans came to the ghetto and asked for 50 young girls to go to work, including 17-year-old Rae. They were taken to the town square where the Germans had also gathered all the Jewish doctors, lawyers, professors, and teachers from the ghetto. As an orchestra played, the Germans shot each one of the "intellectuals." Then the girls were ordered to wash the blood from the cobblestone streets while the Germans danced in the square.

Rae's brother was taken one evening for a similar task. He and 20 other Jewish boys were shot and their bodies burned. "My mother

> "We have the sacred duties to recognize these miracles in our daily lives and to transmit the stories of our past to the next generations."

went in search of him and found my brother burned from the fire, but he was still alive. Some Jews sneaked out, wrapped my brother up in straw and paper, and brought him into the ghetto." Even without medical help, he recovered.

Germans were taking thousands of people from the ghetto at a time. They were murdered and dropped in mass graves. One time it was the elderly, the next time it was the children. Kushner's sister was killed trying to escape one of these "roundups." Her mother was killed in another one.

When only 300 Jews survived, they decided to dig their way out. Every night for three months they dug, packing the dirt between walls and under beds. One stormy autumn night in 1943, they decided to escape. A group of 70 boys went through the tunnel first. "It was pouring and thundering. The boys got out of the tunnel. They became confused and started to run in different directions. We followed a Jewish boy who knew the way to the farms in the area. He was our angel."

The next day, the Germans caught and killed the group of boys who had escaped first. Rae's brother was killed. She, her sister, and her father survived, hiding in the woods for nine months. In 1949, she immigrated to the United States with her new husband. She raised four children. Her family went on to create a highly successful real estate development and management company in which Kushner is still involved today.

"Our life is a miracle. Our children and grandchildren are miracles. We never dreamed that out of the ashes and rubble we would survive to see and build the next generation."

TOM & ANNETTE LANTOS

TOM: MEMBER, U.S. CONGRESS, CALIFORNIA'S 12TH CONGRESSIONAL DISTRICT
ANNETTE: INTERNATIONAL HUMAN RIGHTS ACTIVIST
BOTH WERE SAVED BY SWEDISH HERO RAOUL WALLENBERG

Tom Lantos is the only survivor of the Holocaust ever to be elected to the Congress of the United States. While he now serves as a guardian of the U.S. Constitution, Lantos and his wife, Annette, remember well life without freedom, and they remember the man who gave it back to them. A picture of that man, Swedish diplomat Raoul Wallenberg, hangs on their wall as a constant reminder of one who was a shining light in a dark and depraved world.

Tom and then Annette Tillemann were devoted young friends in Budapest when the Third Reich began its deadly assault on Europe's last remaining Jewish community. As the Jews of Budapest were being forced into ghettos and transported to concentration camps, Wallenberg swung into action. Through his initiatives, not only were Tom's and Annette's lives saved, but also those of a hundred thousand innocent men, women, and children. The Lantoses have fought together for years to focus international attention on the Swedish hero. Because of him, they both escaped the "Final Solution," and they have committed themselves as soldiers in the battle for human rights around the globe.

Wallenberg was sent to Hungary in July 1944 as a Swedish diplomat. His chosen mission was to help the 200,000 Jews remaining in Budapest. He provided Jews with protective passports, granted thousands of Jews Swedish citizenship, and purchased numerous buildings in Budapest declaring them Swedish property protected by international law. He even was known to jump in front of guns leveled at Jews and pull people off trains destined for concentration camps. "He bluffed his way through," says Tom. "He had no real authority. His only authority was his courage. He was absolutely unafraid for himself."

In January 1945, Wallenberg was arrested by the Soviets who were convinced that he was an American spy. He was imprisoned in Moscow. Ten years later, the Soviet government claimed that Wallenberg had died in a U.S.S.R. prison, but legitimate reports of his whereabouts trickled into the West until the early 1980s.

After the war, Tom came to the United States to study economics. He was later joined by Annette, and they were married in 1950. The Lantoses raised two daughters and now have 18 grandchildren.

After three decades as a professor of economics and an international affairs analyst, Tom Lantos was elected to the U.S. Congress where he has served for more than 15 years. The first bill Tom introduced after being elected to office in 1980 made Wallenberg an honorary American citizen. At that time, this honor had been accorded only one other person in American history: Winston Churchill. The Lantoses have worked diligently to focus attention on Wallenberg. Through their efforts, a city block in the nation's capital is now "Raoul Wallenberg Place"; a U.S. postal stamp has been created honoring Wallenberg, and a bust of Wallenberg has been installed as part of a permanent exhibit in the U.S. Capitol. They have also helped to erect Wallenberg memorials in many other cities and have named schools and scholarships after him.

But the most important legacy Raoul Wallenberg left the Lantoses manifests itself in their daily work and devotion to human rights. Tom is cochairman of the 200-member, bipartisan Congressional Human Rights Caucus, while Annette volunteers full-time to accomplish the humanitarian missions of the Caucus. Tom has also cochaired the Congressional Task Force Against Anti-Semitism, served as chairman of the Subcommittee on International Security and Human Rights, and held more than 50 hearings on global human rights issues. In 1995, President Clinton named him the Democratic Congressional Delegate to the United Nations General Assembly.

Tom Lantos regards his office as a platform from which to pursue what he regards as his most important mission in life: creating a more just world where respect for human rights is the central value of every government in the family of civilized nations.

> *"One person can make a difference. There are genuine heroes to illuminate our age."*

EVA LEVINE

MOTHER OF TWO & SURVIVOR OF AUSCHWITZ, KURZBACH, AND BERGEN-BELSEN CONCENTRATION CAMPS

It was hard, says Eva Levine, to choose names for her children. There were so many members of her family who were killed in the Holocaust. There were so many names from which to choose.

Eva, born Eva Keleti in 1921, is from Mukačevo, Czechoslovakia. After the start of the war, that area came under Hungarian rule. She, her sister, Miriam, and her parents were sent to a ghetto and from there to a brick factory.

Within months, Eva and her family were deported to Auschwitz. Eva and her sister, Miriam, were separated from the rest of the family in the "selection" lines. Eva's mother, Josephine, and later her older sister, Ibolya, and her niece all were gassed to death. Ibolya's husband died in a labor camp. Eva's father, Edward, survived for a short time at Auschwitz. She knew he must have been killed when she no longer saw him through the barbed-wire fence separating the women from the men. Eva and Miriam were made slave laborers in the camp.

Every four to six weeks, the laborers had to parade naked before a camp commander. Those who looked ill or too thin were selected for death. As Eva and Miriam passed naked before the infamous Nazi Angel of Death, Josef Mengele, they once again survived selection. "We were very skinny, and we did not know how to make ourselves look better. I pinched my sister's cheeks to make her look more healthy. If you had any pimple or mark on your body, you were sent to the gas chamber. If one of us was chosen for the gas chamber, the other had promised to voluntarily follow. We lived for each other."

"Appreciate life. Live your life day by day, for you can never know what tomorrow will bring."

From Auschwitz, the two were forced to walk to Kurzbach, Germany, to another camp. In midwinter, with few clothes and little food, they dug trenches for the German Army.

The ground was frozen, and they had only their bare hands with which to work.

From Kurzbach, Eva and Miriam were sent to Bergen-Belsen. They were transported by rail in open cattle cars. "While on the train, we were bombed by Allied planes. We hid under the train for protection. I saw some of my friends torn apart and killed by the bombs."

It was from that camp that Eva and Miriam were liberated in April of 1945 by the British. One day after their liberation, Miriam died of starvation and typhoid fever. Eva was taken to Sweden by the Red Cross and immigrated to the United States a year later.

Levine had lost 17 members of her immediate and extended family. She was the only one alive. "After the camps, you feel as if you are dead, and after you start living again, you try not to think about what happened." After the war, she no longer wished for marriage or a family. "How could I put another through what I have endured? The risk was too great should such a horror recur."

But Eva did marry and raise children, Edward Keleti and Miriam Joan, named after her father, mother, and sister. She is also a grandmother.

Eva Levine now lives a life rich with simple day-to-day pleasures. She is thankful, she says, for these simple things: healthy children, sunny days, and food on the table—simple things that, during the war, were not so simple at all.

MAX KARL LIEBMANN

RETIRED BUSINESS EXECUTIVE, STAFF VOLUNTEER AT THE AMERICAN GATHERING
OF JEWISH HOLOCAUST SURVIVORS & SURVIVOR OF GURS CONCENTRATION CAMP

One thing ensured the survival of Max Liebmann: perseverance. Liebmann says, "During the time I was in the concentration camp, there was only one thing on my mind: I'm going to outlive these Nazis! You had to fight and you had to be lucky. I believe that all of us who survived did something to help ourselves."

Liebmann was born an only child in Mannheim, Germany, in 1921. The Nazis came to power during Max's first year in high school, but as early as 1934, he was taunted and beaten by his classmates for being Jewish. Liebmann remained in school as long as he could, until *Kristallnacht*—after that Jews could no longer attend school.

On the night of November 9, 1938, the Nazi discrimination against the Jews turned to violence. It became known as *Kristallnacht,* the night of the broken glass. On that night, over 1,000 synagogues in Germany were destroyed and the remaining Jewish-owned businesses were shattered, including one business in the building where Max, his mother, and his grandmother were living. The rear of the building was rented to a Jewish businessman who sold electrical fixtures. "The mob was smashing all those fixtures. You can imagine how much glass was smashed there. They had a field day."

In 1938, Liebmann's father went to Greece to try to build a new life. He was expelled in 1939 and went to France just before the outbreak of the war. Two weeks before the Allies landed in southern France, his father was caught by the Nazis and deported to Auschwitz where he perished. By the time World War II started in September 1939, Max and his mother were trapped in Germany. In 1940, they were deported to France with more than 6,500 other Jews. "Around 10 o'clock, the Gestapo came and said, 'In the name of the German people, you are under arrest. You have one hour to pack what you can carry.'"

After a three-day train ride, they arrived in Camp Gurs in France. Max spent nearly two years there. In July 1942, Liebmann was permitted to leave the camp and work on a French farm run by Jewish Boy Scouts. A week after he left, all the inmates at Gurs were sent to Auschwitz, his mother among them. She was killed there.

The farm where Liebmann had taken refuge was soon raided. He escaped to the nearby Huguenot village of Le Chambon where he was hidden for four weeks by the French Resistance. They provided him with false identity papers and helped him escape across the Alps to Switzerland. But Max and 35 others were caught by a Swiss patrol and were ordered back to France. Before being pushed across the border, Liebmann was singled out by a Swiss noncommissioned officer who loudly berated him. Liebmann suddenly realized the soldier was giving him a cryptic message with directions on how he and the group might return to Switzerland without being caught. Once released into France, Max pleaded unsuccessfully with the group to try to return to Switzerland. Only one man went with him. Liebmann followed the soldier's directions and found a footpath that led to a Swiss village without being caught. He remained in various camps in Switzerland for five and a half years.

Max Liebmann's girlfriend later joined him in Switzerland. They were married, had a child, and immigrated to the United States, nearly three years after the war's end. Once in the United States, both he and his wife suffered and recovered from tuberculosis. Liebmann worked as a business executive in New York City. Today, he is a staff volunteer at the American Gathering of Jewish Holocaust Survivors.

> "The right to be different is a freedom we all should cherish."

MASHA LOEN

FASHION DESIGNER, AMATEUR POET, HOLOCAUST EDUCATOR
& SURVIVOR OF THE KOVNO GHETTO AND THE STUTTHOF DEATH CAMP

Masha Loen doesn't know how her mother died, but she does know why. Loen's mother was hiding her children in the attic of their peasant house in the Kovno ghetto, and was caught by the Nazis. Loen's father, a tailor, was deported to Dachau in Germany. Masha, her mother, and her two little sisters were deported to Stutthof in Prussia. On arrival, Masha was separated from her family. A couple of days later, she saw them one more time. They were wearing civilian clothing and were being taken away. Masha never saw them again.

Loen was born Mariashka Sapoznikow in 1930 in Kovno, Lithuania. The city was home to over 40,000 Jews before the start of World War II, including Masha, her sister Itale, and her parents. Loen was 11 years old when her family was forced into the Kovno ghetto. Her baby sister, Rosale, was born inside the ghetto walls. The crime that Loen's mother committed was to try to save her children.

In Stutthof, Masha, only 14 years old, endured starvation, slave labor, beatings by camp guards, the last march, and typhus. Finally, Loen was liberated in March 1945. She assisted other survivors in going over the Alps into Italy. Once there, they could obtain help to get to freedom in Palestine. Masha immigrated to the United States with her husband, Cornelius, in 1949.

In California, Masha Loen worked, much like her father, as a clothing designer. She has also worked to keep the memory of Holocaust martyrs alive, both through her writings and through her work as a Holocaust educator. "People can't understand why I work so hard to remember and not allow the world to forget the Holocaust. I cannot and will not forget during what little time I have left in this life."

Since 1978, Loen has worked as a key volunteer with the Martyrs Memorial and Museum of the Holocaust in Los Angeles. She gives frequent lectures to schoolchildren about the Holocaust with a constant message of tolerance and love. She is observant of the annual Jewish holiday each April of Yom Ha Shoah, the remembrance of the 6 million Jews killed in the Holocaust. "This is the time when I visit in my mind the graves of my family and every Jew that perished under the Hitler regime." She also remembers through her poetry:

"Poem from a Child Survivor"

I was a little girl, lost and sad
My mother told me I was not bad,
Then, why the agony and pain
The Nazis inflicted on me with whip and cane?

The question was unanswered because Mother was no more,
They took her away to settle the score.
By hiding her children, she committed a crime,
And that's why they killed her—oh, mother mine.

I wasn't a little girl for long anymore,
I had to survive to settle the score.
The beating did not hurt, the hunger I forgot,
Only one thing was on my mind—to take revenge on the lot.

The time came, and I marched out of hell and pain,
My story I will tell over and over again.
The time has come—you're a statistic no more—
The Martyrs Memorial is settling the score.

Itale, and Rosale, and one-and-one-half million children
Who were killed during the Holocaust years,
In the years to come, when I'm no longer here,
Somebody else will walk by the plaque, and shed for you a tear.

"Don't project hatred. It will only hurt you. Embrace love."

HELEN LUKSENBURG

HOLOCAUST EDUCATOR, VOLUNTEER AT THE U.S. HOLOCAUST MEMORIAL MUSEUM
& CONCENTRATION CAMP SURVIVOR

Helen Luksenburg, then Helen Chilewicz, was born in the town of Sosnowiec on the border between Germany and Poland. That meant that Germans marched into her town very early in the war. And just four days after the Germans arrived, the Polish Army retreated. It was 1939 and Helen was 13 years old.

Restrictions on the Jews included strict curfews, forbidden travel on certain streets, and the rationing of food. Food rations included pork and other nonkosher meats. Most Jews refused to eat that which violated their dietary laws. Appliances, furs, and jewelry were confiscated. Luksenburg's father feared for his family. Helen and other family members went to a different town. "When I returned home two months later, I did not recognize my father. He looked so old and he had lost so much weight."

By 1943, the Germans forced the Jews into a closed ghetto. Helen and her brother were sent to labor camps to work. Upon her return one day, the Sosnowiec ghetto had been liquidated, and her parents and sister were gone. They had been deported to Auschwitz and murdered.

Luksenburg ended up in a sub-camp of Auschwitz. "There were about 600 women. We had to stand at roll call every morning, even if it was 20 below. My number was 79139. We had wooden shoes, no socks.

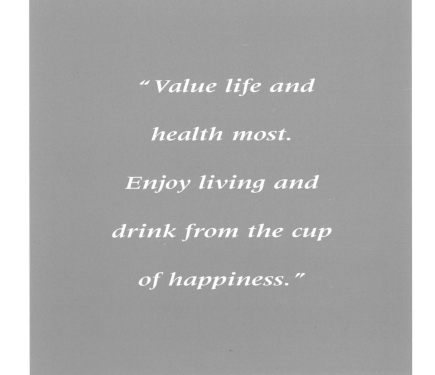

"Value life and health most. Enjoy living and drink from the cup of happiness."

We stuffed them with paper to keep our feet warm. If one person was missing you could stay there for two or three hours. Then you had to work for 12 hours."

Toward the end of the war, Luksenburg and other prisoners were put on open cattle trains. "The Germans didn't know what to do with us. For two weeks in January in weather of 20 degrees below zero, we traveled by rail in open cattle cars. There were 200 people per train car. Eventually, there was more room because people were dying and we were throwing the bodies overboard."

Helen was liberated by the Russians and was sent back to Poland. She returned to Sosnowiec hoping to find her brother, but found no one. She went to Germany, where she met William Luksenburg whom she would later wed. He proposed to her with a men's watch and they held a wedding with money from the sale of an old Ford automobile. They came to America in 1949.

Today Helen Luksenburg is a volunteer at the Holocaust Memorial Museum and she tours schools teaching about the Holocaust. She often reads to students names of 100 people— all family members she lost in the war. She reminds young people that they are the future and mankind's hope. "I believe in peace," Helen says. "and that we are equal. Why should there be such differences, such prejudices, and bigotry?"

BRANKO LUSTIG

COPRODUCER OF THE ACADEMY AWARD–WINNING HOLOCAUST MOVIE, *SCHINDLER'S LIST*, PRODUCER OF SURVIVORS OF THE SHOAH VISUAL HISTORY FOUNDATION & SURVIVOR OF FIVE CONCENTRATION CAMPS

Fascist Hungarians arrested Branko Lustig and his mother in Croatia in 1942. Branko was just 10 years old. Mother and son were sent to Auschwitz, and were immediately separated during the Nazi "selection," the process of dividing those destined for the gas chambers from the able-bodied prisoners. Branko watched as his mother was sent to the left, and he to the right.

Soon after, Branko's sobbing and Croatian speech aroused the attention of a Nazi officer. The officer, too, was Croatian, and had known Branko's father in their hometown of Osijek. The officer allowed the boy to work for him until April of 1944, protecting him from the brutalities of the Nazi camp. Then, the officer left the camp for the Eastern Front.

Branko was sent to nearby Birkenau to work in the coal mines. He was stricken with typhoid fever and soon was loaded onto one of several trucks with other "selected" prisoners, destined for the crematorium. Branko knew what would happen when they reached the ovens. As the caravan traveled along a dry dirt road, a cloud of dust shrouded the trucks. Lustig leapt from the moving vehicle. He spotted a group of naked prisoners running down the road, being herded back to Auschwitz. Unseen by the Nazi guards, Branko stripped and ran with them. The prisoners were taken to the showers, shaven, and tattooed with a number.

In November of 1944, Branko was sent to another camp, Fürstengrube. He survived a midwinter death march from Fürstengrube to Dora. From there, he was sent to Bergen-Belsen. After two and a half years in five different Nazi camps, Branko lay dying in his bunk. He weighed only 50 pounds. Barely alive, he was liberated in the spring of 1945.

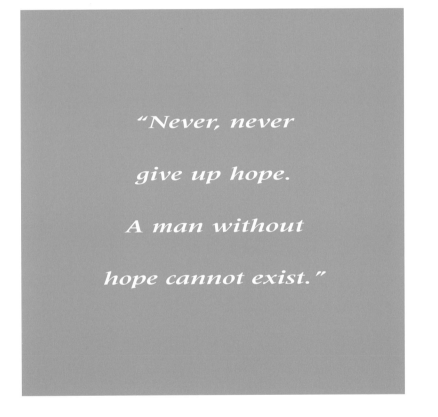

"Never, never give up hope. A man without hope cannot exist."

A former Yugoslavian Army captain was touring the liberated camps, looking for Croatian survivors. As Lustig told the man the details of his capture, the captain recalled having heard a similar story from a woman in the camp several days earlier. That woman was Branko's mother. When the captain returned and informed her that her son was alive and in the same camp, she fainted. Branko and his mother were miraculously reunited. Branko's father was murdered by the Russians in March 1945. He had been fighting for partisans loyal to Yugoslav guerilla leader Marshal Tito.

After the war, Lustig returned to Croatia. There he completed high school and attended the Academy of Film and Television at Zagreb University. He began work at Jadran Films in Zagreb, and stayed there for more than 30 years as a production manager, assistant director, and supervising producer on more than 100 national and foreign coproductions. Beginning in the 1970s, Branko became a principal figure in spearheading the production of American films being shot in Europe, including *Fiddler on the Roof, Winds of War, Sophie's Choice, Tin Drum,* and *War and Remembrance.*

Branko's mother passed away in 1986. The following year, he immigrated to the United States with his wife and daughter. He continued to produce such movies as *The Great Escape I* and *II,* the Emmy Award–winning *Drug Wars: The Camarena Story, Wedlock,* and *Intruders.* In 1992, he was invited to join Steven Spielberg and Jerry Molen in producing the Academy Award–winning *Schindler's List.* Branko Lustig continues his role as a voice from the Holocaust and serves as an executive producer on the Survivors of the Shoah Visual History Foundation, a nonprofit organization dedicated to videotaping eyewitness accounts of the Holocaust all around the world.

MICHEL MARGOSIS

RETIRED RESEARCH CHEMIST, COMMUNITY VOLUNTEER & HOLOCAUST SURVIVOR

Michel Margosis remembers the sweetness of life before the war. Strolling through local fairs, watching movies, and attending Yiddish theater—life as a child in Belgium seemed easy.

Michel was born in September 1928. Eleven years later, World War II began. Belgium was attacked in May 1940. "We heard the sirens shrieking and the sound of explosions throughout the city, and we saw heavy black smoke," Margosis wrote.

Michel's father had already fled persecution during the Russian Revolution. He was interned in Siberia in the 1920s, but he escaped and journeyed by foot to Palestine. He later settled in Belgium as a journalist. He eventually owned and edited two weekly newspapers: one printed in Yiddish and the other one in French. Very outspoken against dictatorships, Margosis's father was alarmed by the events leading up to the Second World War. So, when Brussels was attacked, the Margosis family did not wait for the outcome. They fled.

"We began our saga as we kept one pace ahead of the Nazis. We headed toward the overcrowded railroad station, missed one train connecting to a ship that was subsequently sunk in the Channel on the way to England, but got onto another train headed to the bombed-out city of Mons." They spent seven days and nights traveling, all the while being bombed and strafed, until they arrived in southern France. Michel's father was forced by the events to flee to Portugal. Michel, his mother, and his siblings went into hiding on a farm. After several months, they went to Marseilles again hoping to be reunited with their father.

When the Nazis seized the rest of France, the family headed for Spain. En route by train, they discovered they were traveling with German troops. "My mother with her thick eastern European accent became mute instantaneously and promptly 'learned' sign language, while my brother, sister, and I were audibly indistinguishable from other natives." The next day, they hired two gendarmes as guides who, for a hefty fee, led the family through the 11,000-foot Pyrenees mountains to the safety of Spain. They were arrested two days later by the Spanish Carabineros and incarcerated separately. Later they were released and lived together. In Barcelona, Margosis enlisted in an American program for young refugees and made it to the United States in June 1943. His siblings went to Palestine, and his mother smuggled herself into Portugal to finally rejoin her husband.

Michel's parents came to America in 1946, but it was 10 years later when the whole family was able to be reunited. In the meantime, Margosis attended high school and college in Brooklyn, and enlisted in the U.S. Army. He served as a medic in France during the Korean War. After returning to the States, he worked in pharmaceutical and research labs and as a senior research chemist for the U.S. Food and Drug Administration. He retired in 1990. He is married and has two children.

Michel Margosis now spends his time as a volunteer for a variety of organizations, including the U.S. Holocaust Memorial Museum in Washington, D.C. His memories, he says, are his legacy. "As I have borne witness to the Holocaust," Michel says, "it is now up to you to ensure that it will be remembered."

"One must exult in the ideals and dreams of America and enjoy the richness of life as long as possible."

BENJAMIN MEED

PRESIDENT OF THE AMERICAN GATHERING OF JEWISH HOLOCAUST SURVIVORS & SURVIVOR OF THE WARSAW GHETTO

We have to speak in the name of all those children, of all those relatives, and of all those people who perished." It is the singular mission of Benjamin Meed: to tell and retell the story of the Holocaust, to speak for those who died and to create a record of those who survived.

Meed was born and raised in Warsaw where his family had lived for generations. "My great-grandfather had 18 children, my grandfather had nine children, and I am one of four children. There may be four or five of us left."

During World War II, Benjamin was a slave laborer for the Germans outside the Warsaw ghetto. Inside, he was an active member of the Warsaw underground. Together with his wife, Vladka, they conducted many dangerous missions on both sides of the ghetto walls. They fought in the Warsaw ghetto, avoided deportations, escaped the ghetto, and remained in hiding until the Russian Army entered the city in 1945.

The Meeds arrived in the United States on May 24, 1946, aboard the SS *Marine Perch* with one of the first groups of Holocaust survivors to arrive in New York City. Benjamin had eight dollars in his pocket. They rebuilt their lives from nothing, raised two children, and now have five grandchildren.

Since that time, Meed has become one of the preeminent spokespersons for Holocaust survivors both in America and around the world. He is president and one of the principal founders of the American Gathering of Jewish Holocaust Survivors. The organization represents nearly 100,000 survivors and their families in both the United States and Canada.

Benjamin Meed has been the principal organizer of several major Holocaust survivors' gatherings, including the 1981 gathering in Israel and the 1983 gathering of American survivors in Washington, D.C. The American gathering attracted 20,000 people from across the United States and was the largest survivors' event ever held. With that event, Meed says, "We changed the image of the Holocaust survivor. For years, we were shown as broken people. When we were seen in Washington with the achievement of rebuilding our lives and we were greeted by the President and Congress, people began to listen to us. And the survivors wanted to share their message, not for their sake, but for the sake of future generations.

"As chairman of the event, I had the honor of introducing Ronald Reagan, President of the United States. I felt tremendously privileged. I told of my experience during the Holocaust. As I watched the ghetto burn, I felt abandoned by the entire world. Forty years later, I was introducing President Reagan. I consider that a great moment for me and for survivors because when I spoke, I spoke for them, and when the President spoke, he spoke on behalf of the American people."

Meed has also organized commemorative events in New York City, Miami, and Philadelphia. He is a member of the U.S. Holocaust Memorial Museum Content Committee, and is founder and organizer of the National Registry of Jewish Holocaust Survivors now located in the U.S. Holocaust Memorial Museum. He is often referred to as the "soul" or "neshome" of that institution, but Benjamin Meed says his work is far from complete. "There is so much more to be done. Now, time is my enemy."

> "We must erase indifference from our society. You cannot be indifferent. If you are, you allow the small forces of evil to win."

103

JACOB MELLER

RETIRED BUSINESSMAN & SURVIVOR OF THE KOVNO GHETTO AND DACHAU CONCENTRATION CAMP

After he was liberated in 1945 from the Dachau concentration camp, Jacob Meller did not part with his prison uniform. Still stained with blood and sweat, he kept it with him after liberation and everywhere he went; from Europe to the United States, from Cleveland, Ohio, to Los Angeles, California. It connects him with the past, he says, and does not let him forget.

Meller was born in Kovno, Lithuania, a city that, before World War II, was home to nearly 40,000 Jews. He was in his twenties when the Nazis forced them into the Kovno ghetto. That same year, his mother was taken away, along with 10,000 other Jews, and was led to the infamous Ninth Fort near Kovno. It was the murder site of more than 130,000 Jews from all over Europe.

Jacob and his father were sent to Dachau; his two sisters and four brothers were sent to other camps. During his four years at Dachau, he witnessed the death of his father, and many, many others. Dachau had the evil distinction of being the first Nazi concentration camp, "the perfect training center" for the SS specialists who learned how to persecute the Jews.

Signs of construction were documented as early as March 22, 1933. In 1937, the camp, designed to hold 5,000 prisoners, proved to be too small, as Hitler's Final Solution expanded throughout Europe. Records show that 206,000 prisoners were registered at Dachau between 1933 and 1945. But the exact figures are unknown, because thousands more prisoners were taken there without being registered.

"See and feel the freedom in this country. You have the opportunity to accomplish whatever you desire."

Cruelty was boundless at Dachau. When prisoners stepped on a strip of grass too close to the barbed-wire camp boundary, the SS guards in the watchtowers assassinated them without warning. Flogging, punishment at the stake, and executions were carried out at a predetermined spot known as the Lagerarrest. Dachau was also one of the camps where Nazi doctors conducted medical experiments on defenseless prisoners.

American soldiers liberated the camp on April 29, 1945. Miraculously, all his siblings had been spared in the camps. In 1951, Jacob came to the United States, where, like so many other survivors, he became a part of the American dream. He started a business and raised a family. He is extraordinarily humble. Asked about how he wants to be remembered, he says just as "plain Jacob Meller." Asked about his life's achievements, Meller says, "None. I'm just a survivor of the Holocaust."

Decades later, he still marvels at the freedom and opportunity in America. Decades later, it is still his uniform that is a reminder of the hell he endured and the parents he lost. Now behind a protective cover at the Martyrs Memorial and Museum of the Holocaust in Los Angeles, Jacob Meller's Dachau garment speaks soberly to the nonbeliever who seeks to deny that the Holocaust ever happened. Still, upon closer inspection, the stains on the uniform offer an undeniable, haunting visual refrain when words are simply inadequate.

MELVIN MERMELSTEIN

AUTHOR, LECTURER, BUSINESSMAN, FOUNDER OF THE AUSCHWITZ STUDY FOUNDATION & SURVIVOR OF FOUR CONCENTRATION CAMPS

Tucked away in a quiet section of Huntington Beach, California, are two modest buildings that comprise the Auschwitz Study Foundation. They do not prepare the visitor for their haunting contents: authentic remnants of Hitler's calculated plan to destroy the Jews.

There are Nazi implements of war, torture, and cruelty; photographs; and debris from the European death camps of World War II. Today, this humble museum serves not only as a reminder of the Holocaust, but proof of it. And unfortunately, proof is what Melvin Mermelstein had to have.

Mermelstein is a survivor of four Nazi concentration camps: Auschwitz-Birkenau, Gleiwitz, Gross-Rosen, and Buchenwald. He was liberated at the age of 19.

"Freedom is a powerful word," wrote Mermelstein in his memoirs, *By Bread Alone*. "But to the Jewish inmates at Buchenwald, the words 'liberation' and 'freedom' were immeasurable. On April 11, 1945, at 2:30 p.m., misery, torture, starvation, and death were to come to an end. That was a moment to remember! The moment to be treasured forever and ever.

"While we were free to go, to pass through the gates, we were not free of the barriers of pain, disease, and death. No, we were not free to go. I was not free to go. I was afraid of what the future would reveal and what it might bring. I could not face it and there wasn't any help in sight to ease my struggle and pain. As I stepped from the door of the barracks, I looked at the stacks of dead bodies piled against the building. I was unmoved by the sight. I was numb, without feelings."

Of his family of six, Melvin was the only one to survive. In the summer of 1946, he immigrated to America.

Nearly 40 years after Mermelstein endured the savagery of Hitler's "Final Solution," he waged war against a man once called "the leading anti-Semite in the country," Willis Carto. It was Carto and his California-based Institute for Historical Review that fueled the movement of "Holocaust Denial," an effort to label the Holocaust a "hoax." Carto's *Journal of Historical Review* debated themes such as whether the diary of Anne Frank was a fraud and whether concentration camp gas chambers possessed the capacity to execute 6 million Jews.

Mermelstein, founder of the Auschwitz Study Foundation, Inc., a nonprofit educational foundation dedicated to teaching the events of the Holocaust, became a target of Carto and his "deniers." They mailed Melvin a letter marked "personal," offering him $50,000 to prove that "Jews were gassed in gas chambers at Auschwitz." Mermelstein offered proof of the Nazis' execution gas chambers, then sued after unsuccessfully demanding the institute's $50,000 reward. "I stood up against the 'deniers' of the Holocaust in Los Angeles Superior Court," he explains. Mermelstein won and received a stipulated judgment of $90,000, and a letter of apology to all Auschwitz survivors for the pain and suffering the episode caused.

The court case captured so much attention that it became a national network television movie titled *Never Forget*. It starred Leonard Nimoy as Mermelstein facing the challenges of the revisionists.

Melvin Mermelstein is now married and has four children. He continues to dedicate himself to teaching and understanding the Holocaust. "How was it possible for such madness to have taken place in our time and in such an advanced part of our society? Today," he reminds us, "there are only a few death camp survivors around to offer help and understanding as to how it began and how it was possible for it to succeed."

"Be true to yourself.

Respect your loved ones

and love and respect

your fellowman."

ERNEST W. MICHEL

CHAIRMAN, WORLD GATHERING OF JEWISH HOLOCAUST SURVIVORS IN ISRAEL,
FORMER EXECUTIVE VICE PRESIDENT, NOW EMERITUS, OF NEW YORK UJA-FEDERATION,
AUTHOR, LECTURER & SURVIVOR OF AUSCHWITZ AND BUCHENWALD CONCENTRATION CAMPS

Ernie Michel loves life. "I believe in living life to its fullest," says Michel, who remembers that once, "Death was as close to me as blinking your eyes." He was born in Mannheim, Germany, and survived five and a half years in concentration camps, including Auschwitz and Buchenwald. Ernie's sister survived the war. His parents were gassed at Auschwitz.

Survival, he says, was a matter of luck. "The killings, the gassings, the selections—if they needed workers you weren't gassed, you got another day. It was pure chance." It was chance that saved Michel when he went to the camp infirmary seeking medical attention for an infected head wound suffered at the hands of an SS officer. While in the waiting room, inmates were asked, "Does anyone here have decent handwriting?" Thinking it might be a trick, Ernie reluctantly raised his hand. Having studied calligraphy at his father's insistence, Michel's superior penmanship got him a job writing the death log for inmates to be gassed at Birkenau. His work led to a permanent job in the Auschwitz infirmary.

Caressing a dying friend, Michel silently committed to writing his friend's story if and when he got out of the camp alive. As the end of the war neared, 58,000 inmates were forced to begin a "death march" from Auschwitz in Poland to Germany. Twenty thousand people died on the march. Ernie and two others escaped on a final death march in April 1945 and saved their lives.

Years later, Michel made good on his promise to write his friend's story. His memoirs were published in 1993 in the book *Promises to Keep*. Those promises were to witness, to remember, to speak, and to

never let it happen again. All proceeds from his book sales were donated to the United Jewish Appeal Federation, the organization for which he worked for 45 years. He brought the story of what happened to communities all over the world, "not to just dwell on it, but to show that you can survive and create something positive out of it, namely to live and to bring up families." Michel has a family of three children and six grandchildren.

The zenith of Ernie Michel's postwar career occurred at the 1981 World Gathering of Jewish Holocaust Survivors when he addressed the 6,000 survivors at Yad Vashem. The seeds for this momentous event were sewn while Michel and other prisoners in Auschwitz were celebrating the Passover amid bleak and hopeless surroundings. An excerpt from his address:

"My fellow Survivors: Like many of you, I had a dream. Mine was born in the darkness of Auschwitz. The dream was that one day, if we lived, the Survivors of one of the greatest tragedies in all human history would come and stand together to remind a world that would rather forget, not to let another Holocaust happen to Jews or non-Jews. Once is enough.

"So here we are, all of us sharing memories of a horrifying past, carrying the evidence on our bodies, but proudly standing together to tell a world. We have survived!

"Touched by the madness of our nightmare, we have tried to live normal lives. Scarred by the acid of barbarous hatred, we have tried to give love to our children. Forgotten by a silent world, we have tried to avoid cynicism and despair. Despite all we have known, we affirm life."

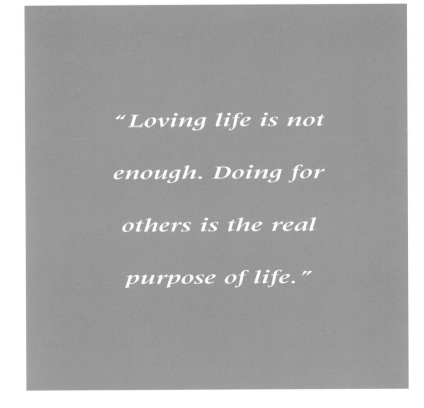

"Loving life is not enough. Doing for others is the real purpose of life."

EDITH MILLMAN

RETIRED RESEARCH SEROLOGIST, TRANSLATOR & SURVIVOR OF THE WARSAW GHETTO

Edith Millman lived in constant fear as she ran from the Gestapo, helped hidden Jews, smuggled supplies, and lived a false identity to save a Jewish life, any life.

Millman was born Edith Greifinger in Bielsko (Silesia), Poland, in 1924. Her father was an executive for Standard Oil Company. Her family moved to Warsaw in 1937, and the war started two years later.

"During the bombing in September 1939, our building was hit. I was injured and spent the rest of the siege in the unventilated subbasement on a pile of coal. Although I was burning with fever, I was refused even a drop of water by the janitor of the building simply because I was Jewish."

The family was forced into the Warsaw ghetto in November 1940. The ghetto was established in a dilapidated section of Warsaw and was surrounded by a 10-foot-high brick wall, topped with barbed wire. The ghetto held 450,000 Jews, one third of the entire prewar population of Warsaw. In the second half of 1942, the daily food rations supplied only 180 calories per person.

Edith worked in the ghetto collecting food, clothing, and money for the most needy people in the tenements. "I vividly remember a 'spoon campaign,' where people were asked to contribute a spoon of flour, cereal, or sugar toward a general collection." She also joined secret study groups. "Since these classes were illegal, we met at different places and, in constant fear of discovery, devised all kinds of cover-ups. When studying, we gathered around a small carbide lamp that was our only source of heat and light. Immersion in studies was a means of escape from the horrid reality of our lives."

Between July and September of 1942, there were selections and deportations from the ghetto. Between 6,000 and 10,000 Jews were sent daily to Treblinka and killed. "Active resistance was discouraged because of collective punishments and ignorance of the planned 'Final Solution.' We were sure that the Allies would win and that liberation was only a matter of time."

Millman escaped to the Aryan section of Warsaw at the end of 1942 and obtained false identity papers. She posed as a Polish gentile and, because of her knowledge of the German language, got a job at the railway where she was able to steal blank railroad identity cards and supplementary food stamps for the Polish underground. Edith also stole coal from the trains to help a Jewish family in hiding.

"Surviving was frequently based on pure luck. At other times, when I was numb to fear, chutzpah took over." Once, when caught by a Polish policeman, she broke from his grasp and ran across the street to a German military policeman. Showing her false identity card, she asked for help. The German soldier angrily confronted the policeman, and told him to look for Jews and bandits and not to bother pretty girls.

In 1944, Millman was liberated from her double life by the Russian Army's advances on the Germans. By war's end, only five people in her extended family were alive. Forty-eight had perished.

After the war, Edith Millman came to the United States where she attended college and worked as a research serologist and later as a translator and abstractor of foreign medical articles.

She is married, has two children, and volunteers at the Holocaust Oral History Archives at Gratz College in Philadelphia, Pennsylvania. The archives include 750 audiotaped interviews with survivors, liberators, rescuers, and witnesses to the tragedies of the Holocaust.

> *"Approach people and situations with an open mind; never prejudge anybody because of their looks, race, or religion. Try to understand the differences among people and learn from it."*

ANN & PAUL MONKA

PAUL: RETIRED MECHANICAL ENGINEER AND MANUFACTURER OF RADAR COMPONENTS
BOTH ARE MEMBERS OF THE HOLOCAUST REMEMBRANCE AND EDUCATION COUNCIL OF METROWEST
AND THE METROWEST SPEAKERS BUREAU & SURVIVORS OF THE HOLOCAUST

Ann and Paul Monka did not meet until after the war, but their lives during the Holocaust were similarly harrowing. Both lived in Poland and both witnessed the suffering of Jews at the hands of the Nazis.

Ann was 11 years old when the Nazis occupied the city of Lida in Poland. Lida was not far from the city of Minsk in Belorussia. When the Nazis invaded Poland, Russian armies occupied Lida, dividing Poland into two parts. But when Germany invaded Russia in June 1941, the city and the fate of the Jewish population fell victim to the Nazis.

On May 8, 1942, the Nazis took the entire Jewish population out of Lida. The children, the sick, and the elderly were marched 300 at a time to the woods outside the city. Nazis told them to undress, and then shot them. Their bodies fell into mass graves. They executed 6,700 innocent people.

Ann lost her grandmother, uncles, aunts, cousins, and friends in the slaughters.

Ann's father, brother, and sister were put in a railcar destined for Majdanek concentration camp, but escaped by jumping from the train. Ann and her mother hid in their attic during a Nazi selection, then slipped out at night, and took refuge in the forest. Ann and her mother spent three weeks hiding in the woods. She says she will never forget surviving on berries and sleeping on the cold, hard ground until they stumbled on a partisan group organized by Tuvia Bielski, a Jewish commander and hero. Bielski took in children, men and women, the young and old, who escaped the Nazi atrocities. Ann and her mother, in a tearful and happy reunion, were rejoined by her father and siblings who escaped from the train. The family lived in the partisan camp in the forest for two years and was liberated by the Russian Army in 1944.

Paul, meanwhile, was fighting in the Polish underground. Paul was from the Polish city of Bendzin near the German border. His town had a population of 65,000—45,000 of them were Jewish. The third day of the war, the Nazis occupied the city and began a campaign of terror against the Jews.

"The Nazis surrounded the main synagogue and burned it down while people were inside praying. They executed those who tried to escape. Eight hundred people were killed, among them one of my best childhood friends. We watched this execution from the roof of our building. Suddenly, fear overwhelmed me. I started to scream."

Paul worked in a factory that produced parts for tanks and planes. There he met people from the Polish underground and joined them. He was arrested and tortured, but managed to get away. The underground organization rescued Paul's brother from the camps as well as many others. At the war's end, Paul became a captain in the Polish Army, then achieved the rank of lieutenant colonel. He left Poland in 1947. He and Ann met in 1951 in the United States and they were married. They have three children and seven grandchildren.

The Monkas both frequently lecture on their experiences. "We feel it is important to share and retrace our tragic past so that our children and grandchildren may have a better future."

"Participate in the peaceful future of this great nation."

BILL MORGAN

REAL ESTATE EXECUTIVE, PHILANTHROPIST & SURVIVOR OF THE STANISLAWOW GHETTO

The Nazis forced Bill Morgan to dig graves for Jews assembled in a cemetery, awaiting execution by a sniper's bullet. He decided to run for his life.

Morgan, born Wolf Marguiles, was 16 years old. He was one of seven children in a poor Jewish family in the Ukraine, part of Poland at the onset of World War II.

The Jews in the Stanislawow ghetto were suffering from hunger and disease. Streets were littered with dead people. They were dying faster than they could be buried. And to hurry up the killing process, the Germans would drive into the ghetto at night, run from house to house grabbing people, force them on trucks, and haul them straight to the cemetery where they shot them one by one and dumped them into mass graves.

"I saw it with my own eyes because I was digging those graves. I was sure I was next because they did not want any eyewitnesses," says Morgan.

"I slipped behind a tombstone and waited for a chance to take off. When that moment came, I ran back to the ghetto, through the back streets. I remember walking into the house and telling my family what I had seen. I said, 'They are killing us all! I am leaving! I am not going to wait to be shot. I might as well get shot on the run!' Mother pleaded, 'You can't leave. You are the only one that brings us food.' I told her that I had to leave."

Morgan hugged his family and said good-bye. Then his father laid his hand on young Bill's head and said, "Son, be sure you say Kaddish for us. When we meet in heaven, you can tell us all about it." Certain that his family died in that ghetto, Morgan does say Kaddish for them. (Kaddish is the Hebrew prayer recited in memory of the dead.) Since the date they perished is unknown to Bill, he recites Kaddish every March 3, the official dedication date of the Holocaust Museum Houston.

That night, Morgan jumped the ghetto fence and boarded a train. With his perfect Polish and Ukrainian and his lack of Semitic features, he posed as a non-Jew under the assumed name of Stephan Chesnowsky. It was the first of several false identities for Bill. This one got him a job on a farm. Each breath could have been his last if the farmers discovered he was a Jew.

At the war's end, Bill left Poland and waited four years in Germany to immigrate to America. He arrived in 1949 and set out for California. On his way, his car broke down in Houston and he didn't have enough money to fix it. So, he got a job selling shoes. He taught himself to speak English. If he made a dollar, he spent only 10 cents and saved the rest. Morgan went from selling shoes, to owning a snack bar, to selling meat from the trunk of his car, to owning a meat-packing house.

In 1960, he founded a construction company. Bill knew nothing about the business, but often took blueprints home at night to study them. Today, the Morgan Group, Inc., is a multistate, multimillion-dollar housing construction company not only bearing his name, but also employing the talents of his three sons. Morgan and his wife, Shirley, raised three sons and two daughters.

Bill Morgan is intensely dedicated to keeping the remembrance message alive. He played a fundamental role in establishing the Holocaust Museum Houston. He is a major supporter and the residing chairman. And he never forgets his roots. "If God would give me back the years, I would give it back to the country, to the community, and to the people of America who gave me a break."

"If you can't make it in America, you can't make it anywhere."

MIRIAM OSTER

RETIRED REAL ESTATE DEVELOPER & SURVIVOR OF THE LODZ GHETTO AND NAZI CONCENTRATION CAMPS

Her babies were ages three and a half and one when the Nazis took them. Little Jocheved and Avremele were placed in a children's transport from the Lodz ghetto and killed in the Polish death camp at Chelmno. "How," wonders Miriam Oster, "how did we live through such a tragedy and go on with our lives?"

Miriam was from Lodz, as was her husband, Bernard Ostrowiecki Oster. They were married in 1936. In 1939, the Jews were forced into the one small, dilapidated part of the city. Oster recalls how in the Lodz ghetto, hunger and death were all around them.

The Germans began their plan to deport the very young and old. People were told that their loved ones were being sent to work. When the transports arrived at the concentration camps, everyone was gassed. The ghetto population shrank noticeably each day as more and more people were deported. Oster's most unforgettable moment in the ghetto was when the Nazis took away the little children. Among those deported on September 5, 1942, were her first- and second-born children.

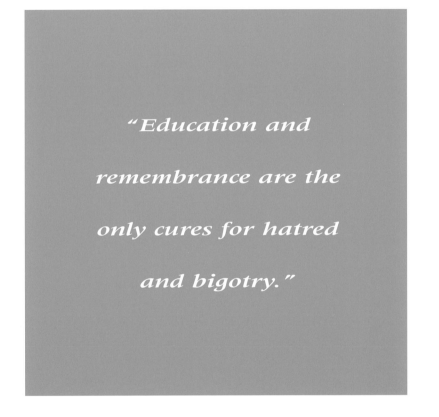

"Education and remembrance are the only cures for hatred and bigotry."

Conditions in the ghetto grew more and more difficult. Jews' property was confiscated by the German forces and they were beaten. "I was viciously beaten. My mother died of hunger in the ghetto. The last words from her lips were 'The Russians.'"

The Germans, knowing the Russians were not far from Warsaw, began grabbing Jews from the streets and from their homes. They were liquidating the ghetto, and sending the last 500 Jews in Lodz to Auschwitz and Birkenau. Oster and her husband were on that transport to Birkenau and were then sent to Stutthof to work for the Wehrmacht (German Army). "We did all kinds of labor. This was a terrible death camp. Of our group of 500 people, only 270 were left. We dropped like flies from the beatings and hunger."

Miriam was able to see her husband every day in the adjacent camp, though they were separated by barbed wire. They were sent to Dresden to work in a factory in December 1944. Then, early in 1945, the Allies bombed Dresden. "Miraculously, we got out alive. By spring, the Russians were moving in, and the prisoners were forced on a death march in April. "They hurried us day and night on foot without food in the direction of Czechoslovakia. The last days were terrible. Even as we saw liberation was near, half of us died on the death march."

The small group of surviving prisoners arrived in Theresienstadt, Czechoslovakia. They were liberated by the Russians on May 8, 1945.

Oster and her husband regained their strength and started to rebuild their lives. They immigrated to America in 1952 and they had two more children, Abe and Daniel. The Osters became very successful real estate developers. They were completing a luxury condominium complex in New Jersey known as the Atrium, and were preparing to move into a suite they had saved for themselves on the 18th floor. Shortly before they were to move, Miriam's husband died suddenly. They had selected the 18th floor, because the number 18 signifies life in Hebrew.

Their children have since become leaders in the creation of A Living Memorial to the Holocaust-Museum of Jewish Heritage in New York City— a museum, they say, that will "show us the richness and splendor of Jewish life, a life of Yiddishkeit that was lost in the Holocaust."

LEOPOLD PAGE

BUSINESSMAN, COMMUNITY LEADER & THE SINGULAR CATALYST FOR THE *SCHINDLER'S LIST* STORY

While in Beverly Hills in October 1980, acclaimed Australian novelist Thomas Keneally stopped at the leather goods store of Leopold (Pfefferberg) Page, to get his briefcase repaired. For Page, this customer was the encounter he had been awaiting for nearly 40 years. This was the man who would tell his story, the story of hundreds of other Jews, and the story of a German Catholic industrialist named Oskar Schindler.

Keneally went on to write the best-selling book, *Schindler's List,* which was published in November 1982 and sold more than 5 million copies in 19 different languages. The book received the distinguished English literary award, the Booker Prize, and later became the basis of Steven Spielberg's production of *Schindler's List.* The movie opened to outstanding reviews and has been seen by more than 350 million people worldwide. Page served as a consultant for the film and is portrayed as Leopold Pfefferberg. The movie went on to win seven Academy Awards including Best Director and Best Picture.

Leopold and his wife, Ludmila, were both "Schindler Jews," two of more than 1,300 Jews who were saved from the Holocaust when Schindler put their names on his now-famous "list" of workers needed for his factories.

Before the war in 1936, Leopold Pfefferberg had earned a master's degree from the Jagiellonian University in Krakow, one of the most prestigious universities in Europe. He became a high school professor and taught until the war broke out in September 1939. He then joined the Polish Army with the rank of lieutenant and fought against the Nazis. Soon after, he was wounded and interned, but subsequently escaped and returned to teaching until January 1, 1940, when all schools were closed by the Nazis.

He and Ludmila married in war-torn Krakow in July of that year. Both were sent to the Krakow ghetto in 1941, and in March 1943, after they had lost their entire families, they were interned in the Nazi concentration camp Plaszow. Before the order came to liquidate Plaszow in November 1944, Schindler created his now-famous "list" and transported his workers to Brünnlitz to work in his munitions factory until liberation on May 8, 1945.

In April 1947, the Pfefferbergs decided to immigrate to the United States. Before leaving, Leopold, also known as Poldek, promised Oskar Schindler that, because of his humanitarian deeds, he would try to make Schindler's name a household word. The two men forged a lifelong friendship.

Poldek remembers the last time he saw Schindler in May 1973 when they met in Israel for the 25th anniversary of Israel's Independence. Schindler told Poldek that when he died, his wish was to be buried in Jerusalem. Schindler died the following year in October 1974, in Germany. With the permission of the Israeli and German governments, it was arranged for Schindler's body to be transferred to Jerusalem where he was buried in a Catholic cemetery on the hill of Mount Zion, with full honors as a "Righteous Gentile" for saving more than 1,300 Jewish lives.

As Thomas Keneally stated, "Oskar Schindler saved the lives of Poldek and Mila, but they gave Oskar Schindler immortality."

Leopold and Ludmila Page continue to tell Schindler's story today, speaking to audiences around the world. Leopold has also been instrumental in the creation of the Los Angeles Holocaust Monument in Pan Pacific Park, which was dedicated in April 1992, in memory of the 6 million Jews. Today, Page is active in The "1939" Club, a prestigious survivors' organization in Los Angeles. He also continues to volunteer for various organizations such as the Boy Scouts of America, the Beverly Hills Chamber of Commerce, and others for which he has been publicly honored.

It is important to Page that his family carry the torch. "Our heritage must be passed to our children, Marie and Fred, and his wife, Judy, and our grandchildren, Samantha and Matthew. They will ensure our legacy for the future."

> *"Even in the darkest moments of history, people of different races, religions, and nationalities can find respect and compassion for one another."*

MURRAY PANTIRER

REAL ESTATE DEVELOPER, MEMBER OF THE U.S. HOLOCAUST MEMORIAL COUNCIL, PHILANTHROPIST & SURVIVOR OF GROSS-ROSEN CONCENTRATION CAMP, AND A SCHINDLER JEW

At 19, Murray Pantirer was awaiting death in the Gross-Rosen concentration camp. Shortly before he was to be killed, he was transferred to Brünnlitz, Czechoslovakia, after his name somehow appeared on the now-famous "Schindler's List."

Oskar Schindler was a German industrialist who rescued 1,300 Jews from the jaws of destruction by employing them in his factories during the war. Pantirer does not know how he came to be listed as a sheet metal worker and a Schindler employee. He says an angel marked his name and put it on that list.

The improbable rescue of Pantirer and other Jews was the subject of Steven Spielberg's 1993 award-winning film, *Schindler's List*, in which Murray was invited to appear. He and other Schindler survivors gathered in Israel in an epilogue scene at Oskar Schindler's grave site. Spielberg called the movie a "tribute to a time that must never be forgotten."

Since his arrival in America in 1949, Murray Pantirer, too, has worked to ensure that no one forgets the Holocaust. Through his philanthropy and community work, he keeps alive the memory of the eight family members he lost to Nazi terrorism, including his parents, Bella, 41 and Lezur, 42; his two sisters, Ester, 12, and Rachel, 7; and four brothers: Herschel, 21; Josef, 15; Mordhi, 15; and Israel David, 9. The family lived in Krakow before the war.

After the war, Pantirer settled on the East Coast and became the cofounder of a successful real estate development company. He has received a long list of honors and awards for his civic activities and contributions. Pantirer was appointed by President Reagan as a member of the U.S. Holocaust Council, and reappointed by President Bush to remain in the position until 1998. Murray also serves as chairman of the Holocaust Resource Center at Kean College in Union, New Jersey, and is a member of the New Jersey Advisory Council on Holocaust Education in the public schools.

Murray Pantirer is a founding member of the U.S. Holocaust Memorial Museum in Washington, D.C., a fellow of Yad Vashem in Jerusalem, a member of the board of the American Gathering of Jewish Holocaust Survivors, and sits on the Board of Governors of the Great Synagogue of Jerusalem. He also spearheaded the fund-raising campaign to build the Holocaust statue at Liberty State Park in New Jersey.

Pantirer is a recipient of a Doctor of Law degree from the Rabbinical College of America, and is past president of the Jewish Educational Center in Elizabeth, New Jersey. In May of 1995, he was awarded an honorary doctorate of Humane Letters from Kean College in Union, New Jersey.

Those who have had the opportunity to know Murray Pantirer say he is a man of few words; rather, he speaks with his deeds. A simple saying from the Talmud, the body of Jewish civil and religious law, holds great meaning for Pantirer. It is also the saying that was engraved inside a ring made from the gold in the teeth of Schindler Jews. It was presented to Oskar Schindler on the last day of World War II. It says:

"He who saves

a single soul,

saves the

world entire."

MAURICE PECHMAN

CERAMICS COMPANY OWNER & SURVIVOR OF AUSCHWITZ AND SACHSENHAUSEN CONCENTRATION CAMPS

Maurice Pechman describes himself as a troublemaker when he was young. The spunk and spontaneity of a young boy who would leave a snail on his teacher's desk were just what he would need to escape again and again from death at the hands of the Nazis.

Pechman was born in the Polish town of Jaworow. His family lived in a one-room home. There was no electricity and often not enough food. The family of eight, including four older brothers and a younger sister, was very close.

The Pechman family was living in Krakow when Germany invaded Poland. They fled to a small village thinking they would be safe there, but they were not. "German soldiers ordered everyone at gunpoint into the wagons. Then they took us into the fields, to a huge pit. The SS began shooting people in the back of the head. I was in the last row. People were screaming, crying, and falling into the pit. But sometimes the victim wasn't dead yet and you would hear his horrifying moans and then more shots. I ran toward the woods as fast as I could. I hid and they didn't catch me. I never saw my parents again. I know they were killed at that pit."

Maurice went to Tarnow to find an older brother who he was told was still alive. He learned that his brother, on his way to be married, was stopped by the Gestapo at the gate to the Tarnow ghetto. His brother was arrested and then shot for not wearing the armband that identified him as a Jew.

In Tarnow, Pechman obtained false identity papers from the Jewish underground. He would try to escape by train, posing as Jan

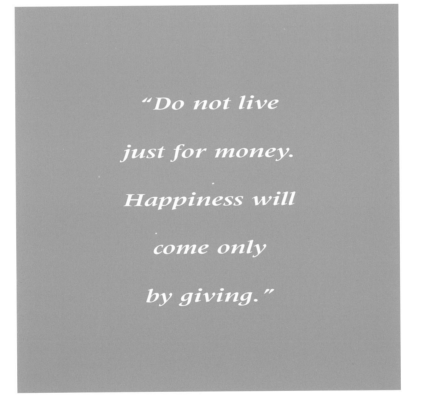

"Do not live just for money. Happiness will come only by giving."

Zachwala, a Christian Pole. At the Tarnow train station, German and Polish police were searching for Jews who might be trying to escape." 'Papers!' demanded an officer. I gave him my papers. He told me to wait with about 50 other people. I was terrified. I wanted to run away but I was trapped. A young boy was standing near me and begged me to carry a valise for him. He insisted that it only contained salami and that he'd give me one later as payment. When the police finally called us, they ordered me to open the valise. I did. It was full of anti-Nazi leaflets and papers. They beat me so hard for two weeks that my body was black with bruises. There was no white skin left."

Pechman, who was not quite 15, was sent to Auschwitz. His weight dropped to 75 pounds. In 1944, he was transferred to Sachsenhausen-Oranienburg, but once Russian troops began closing in, the Germans sent the prisoners on a death march. Thousands died. Maurice escaped and hid in the woods. He was liberated three days later and discovered that one of his brothers had survived Auschwitz. The rest of his family had perished.

Maurice Pechman arrived in New York at the age of 21. "After all I'd been through, I wasn't afraid of anything," says Pechman. "I saw the opportunity in this country and I went for it." His first taste of this American opportunity came when he took a job as a Fuller brush man. He went on to sell everything from sewing machines to freezers. Eventually, he got into ceramics. He built the business empire of Maurice Ceramics, a label that is embossed and fired into the clay of millions of dollars' worth of ceramics each year.

ABE RESNICK

REAL ESTATE DEVELOPER, FOUNDING MEMBER OF THE HOLOCAUST MEMORIAL
IN MIAMI BEACH, MEMBER OF THE U.S. HOLOCAUST MEMORIAL COUNCIL &
SURVIVOR OF THE KOVNO GHETTO AND LIBERATOR OF SACHSENHAUSEN CONCENTRATION CAMP

Abe Resnick is a survivor, not once, but twice, and that is only the beginning of his legacy.

He is a Holocaust survivor, liberator of a concentration camp, a Cuban refugee, a prominent developer who never went to college, a man who first ran for political office at age 61 and then served four terms, a community leader, a philanthropist, and a builder of a synagogue and Holocaust memorial. And his friends know him simply as a soft-spoken man of Old World charm, shy but warm.

Resnick, born in 1924 as Abraham Resnikowitz, was from the Lithuanian town of Rokishki, a town of 7,000, half of whom were Jewish. He was schooled in his hometown, then as a teenager went to Lithuania's capital city of Kovno to a gymnasium, a private institute of higher learning. After eight years there, his plan was to apply to medical school at a university in Italy. He never had the chance.

The Nazis attacked Russia and Lithuania in 1941. Kovno was bombed. Resnick tried to return home, but could not. He returned to his apartment in Kovno, where his grandmother, aunt, and uncle also lived. They were forced into the Kovno ghetto, an area of about two square miles that held 38,000 Jews.

"Soon I heard that the Nazis needed 500 educated people for a special assignment with a promised reward of extra food. I tried to volunteer but was too late as the quota was quickly filled. I was disappointed at a missed opportunity but I later discovered that the special assignment was an execution. The Nazis sought to cleanse the ghetto of its most educated prisoners."

Nazis systematically murdered, raped, and hanged Jews. Thousands were sent to death camps and, by 1944, Resnick was one of only 7,000 Jews left in the ghetto. The Nazis began to liquidate the ghetto, and Resnick and several comrades planned their escape. Abe hid in an abandoned house and at night cut through the barbed wire surrounding the ghetto and ran into the woods. He joined the partisans in Lithuania and later joined the Russian Army, hoping to fight the Nazis and avenge the deaths of all those in his family. As a Russian soldier, he participated in the liberation of Berlin and Sachsenhausen concentration camp.

In 1947, Abe escaped the Russian Army and left Berlin to join relatives in Cuba. There he spent 13 productive years. He married, had two sons, and became a prominent business and community leader.

In 1959, Fidel Castro's rise to power as the head of the Communist regime in Cuba forced Resnick to flee again. He and his family arrived in Miami Beach in 1960. By 1965, he was a major property owner and became one of the country's first condominium developers.

Abe Resnick also became involved in civic affairs. Among other things, he built a synagogue in his father's memory, served four terms as city commissioner and vice-mayor for Miami Beach, and spearheaded the construction of the Miami Beach Holocaust Memorial.

"Do not do to others what you do not want done unto yourself."

FRED ROER

RETIRED WAREHOUSE MANAGER & SURVIVOR OF THE LODZ GHETTO AND SEVERAL CONCENTRATION CAMPS

Fred Roer wrote letters in code to his sister-in-law, requesting that she send bread. She did, and she would also hide money inside it. That's just one of the ways this German Jew survived one of the four Nazi concentration camps.

Roer was 20 when he, his brother, and his mother were forced to leave their hometown of Kerpen, Germany. It was 1941 and they were headed for the ghetto in Lodz. Fred's father had died in an accident years earlier.

The Roer family joined a sea of others also forced from their homes. It was then, in the mass of suffering, that Fred was separated from this family forever.

Shortly after arriving in Lodz, Roer was sent to the notorious Poznan slave labor camp. There he dug irrigation ditches and helped to excavate a large man-made lake from 1941 to 1943. Early on, Fred received packages from his sister-in-law in Germany. Later, the Nazis confiscated the packages and ordered the prisoners to write friends for money. The Gestapo then confiscated the money, too. The inmates discovered that farmers in the area secretly stored potatoes and beets in holes covered with straw. Sometimes, prisoners would slip away into the fields, retrieve the vegetables, and trap chickens, rabbits, birds, and geese.

From Poznan, Fred was sent to another slave labor camp, and then to Auschwitz to work in an underground coal mine. Prisoners did what they could to sabotage the Nazi war machine: damage equipment, hurl loaded wagons down hills, mix rocks with coal, and shred equipment wires, all the while facing the threat of being shot in the head if discovered. Roer labored in the coal mines at Auschwitz until January 1945. His next destination was the Gross-Rosen slave labor camp. From there, Fred was sent to the Regensburg camp in southern Germany.

In the spring of 1945, Roer and hundreds of other prisoners were forced on a death march from Regensburg to the brutal camp of Mauthausen in Austria. The Mauthausen stone quarries had become known as places of great torture and death. They never reached the quarries, but instead were liberated by the U.S. Army at the German-Austrian border near Bad Reichenhall.

Fred Roer was now free, but alone. He immigrated to the United States in 1949 with only $21 in his pocket.

Adjusting to a new life was not easy, he recalls. But the taste of freedom surpassed any challenges Fred would face in this land of opportunity. Today, Roer is a retired warehouse manager and lives a quiet life with his family in Seattle. He enjoys simple things and says he is happy to be alive. In fact, he says, it is everything to be alive.

In 1992, Roer and his wife went to the Yad Vashem Archives in Israel. In a book in which the Nazis kept records, they found the name of his brother. From Lodz, his brother was sent to Auschwitz, then to Dora where he was killed two months before the end of the war. Though they had been in Auschwitz at the same time, Fred never saw him or heard about him while there. He believes his mother also perished in Auschwitz.

> *"Never discriminate or hate anybody for any reason. Treat every human being the way you would want to be treated."*

MANCI, HENRY & ALEXANDER ROSNER

SURVIVORS OF PLASZOW LABOR CAMP, SCHINDLER JEWS,
THE VIOLINIST FAMILY WHO ACHIEVED FAME IN THE MOVIE *SCHINDLER'S LIST*
ALEXANDER: FOUNDER OF CUSTOM SOUND SYSTEM COMPANY

To live, the body puts itself into a defensive, energy-conserving survival mode, while the heart locks itself up for safekeeping." That was the recipe for survival for Alexander Rosner, a boy of four when World War II began. "I had my father with his violin to protect me. He was defiant in the face of danger, constantly insisting that everything was going to be all right, and I believed him," says Alexander.

Alexander's parents were Marianne (known as Manci) and Henry Rosner. Henry was a violinist who played professionally in well-known cafes, hotels, and resorts all over Europe until Poland fell to the Nazis in 1939. In 1942, the Rosners, their young son, and Henry's two brothers were sent to the Plaszow forced labor camp. There, Henry and his brother, Poldek, an accordionist, were required to play for the camp commandant, Amon Goeth. They entertained at the commandant's dinner parties, and were frequently called upon to play lullabies for Goeth at his villa. Henry played on a fine violin, crafted in 1890 by a master Italian instrument maker in Turin. Henry had bought it in Vienna in 1928.

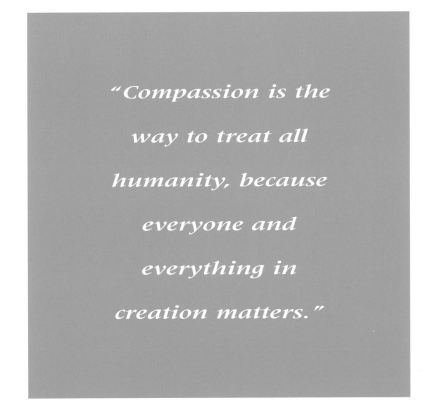

"Compassion is the way to treat all humanity, because everyone and everything in creation matters."

It was at Goeth's villa that the German industrialist Oskar Schindler was a frequent dinner guest and, like Goeth, enjoyed the Rosners' music. Schindler is credited with saving the lives of 1,300 Jews whom he employed in his factories during the war. So taken was Schindler with the Rosners' talents that he added the names of the entire Rosner family to his now-famous list of workers needed for his Brünnlitz munitions plant.

Henry's violin never made it to the sanctuary of Schindler's factory. It was taken from Henry at the Gross-Rosen transit camp along the way.

Henry told the SS guard who confiscated it that the "fiddle," as well as Poldek's accordion, were the property of Oskar Schindler. Schindler later ransomed the instruments and presented the violin to Manci on the factory floor at Brünnlitz. By that time, Henry and the young Alexander had been sent to Dachau. They survived until liberation and went to a prearranged meeting place. The family and the violin were reunited in Munich in the autumn of 1945.

After immigrating to the United States, Henry resumed his career as a professional musician, playing at some of New York City's finest restaurants and hotels, still with his Italian violin. Henry played the instrument for more than 66 years. Through the generosity of fellow Schindler Jews, Henry's violin became part of a permanent collection at the U.S. Holocaust Memorial Museum. Henry died in 1995.

After the war, Henry's son Alexander was educated in the United States, served in the U.S. Navy, and then worked in the defense industry for eight years. He then made a profession out of his love for music and founded a company that specializes in the design and construction of custom audio and video systems for homes, commercial establishments, performing arts spaces, and houses of worship, all over the world. Alexander has three children. His mother, Manci, lives nearby.

The Rosner family's poignant story is highlighted in the 1993 award-winning movie *Schindler's List*. Alexander and his parents took part in the filming of the movie's closing scenes in Jerusalem at the site of Oskar Schindler's grave. Since that time, Alexander has been speaking publicly in high schools and in places of worship about hatred, bigotry, and the Holocaust.

IRVING SCHAFFER

RETIRED PIANO TECHNICIAN & SURVIVOR OF AUSCHWITZ, THE WARSAW GHETTO, A DEATH MARCH FROM POLAND TO GERMANY, AND THE DACHAU AND LANDSBERG CONCENTRATION CAMPS

Do not give up. Be strong and we will meet again," said Irving Schaffer's father as they embraced for the last time at Auschwitz. They did not meet again. His father, mother, two brothers, and two sisters were murdered at Auschwitz. Only Irving and another brother survived.

Schaffer was 14 in 1944 when he was taken from the ghetto in his hometown of Chust, Czechoslovakia, and sent to Auschwitz. After the Warsaw ghetto was bombed by the Germans, he was among those prisoners transported to Warsaw and forced to clean the ghetto. All recoverable items were collected and sent to Germany to be reused.

The Warsaw ghetto was liquidated when the Russians began shelling the area. Schaffer was among a large group of prisoners sent on a death march to Germany. He watched as so many of his comrades, weakened by hunger, thirst, and disease, fell by the road. Those too weak to continue were shot by Nazi guards. Schaffer and other prisoners were selected to bury the dead. "I can still visualize where we buried some of their bodies. I remember one man who we buried on top stretched out his hand and said to me, 'Please don't bury me. I am still alive.'" The death march continued.

"While we were marching, many prisoners jumped off the bridges into the water. The SS sent German shepherd dogs after them and killed them once they were found. Those who tried to run were shot." The prisoners were ordered to stop for the night in an open field near a lake. Schaffer remembers how some prisoners began to dig up the ground with their spoons, digging deep enough to find water. "Our lips were black as coal from dehydration and it felt so good to have a little water. I remember taking handfuls of water with stones and sand and swallowing whatever I had in my hands."

The following day, the prisoners reached the German-Polish border and waited in the forest for a freight train. They were then stuffed into boxcars—110 prisoners per car—and the tiny train windows were boarded up. "The SS told us to take a deep breath and hold it so they could fit one more person in the car." There was little air, no food, and no water. Schaffer was one of only six prisoners to survive the train trip to yet another death camp, Dachau.

At Dachau, Irving remembers seeing dead bodies everywhere. "It was like a floor of just bodies." Schaffer collapsed. "When I came to, I also wanted to die, but I remembered the words of my father."

From there, Schaffer was placed on a truck to Landsberg where he was to work in a munitions factory. Caught stealing potatoes from a bunker, Schaffer was chained and severely beaten. He was given two days to recuperate in his barracks and was then sent back to work, this time at another camp.

As the end of the war neared, the camp was to be liquidated. The prisoners were being transported by train. Suddenly, U.S. forces bombed the train Irving was in by mistake while chasing another German train. An SS commandant declared that the prisoners were free to go. Schaffer began to run. He turned around as some of his comrades fell. "Get up! Run!" he cried to them, and then realized the SS were chasing and shooting at them. Schaffer again remembered the words of his father. He was caught and brutally beaten by the Nazis.

Schaffer awoke in a hospital three days later. He had been in a coma and weighed 65 pounds. He had been liberated by the Americans. After three weeks, he left the hospital to search for his family. He found his brother alive.

In 1947, Irving Schaffer immigrated to the United States. He and his wife have three children and three grandchildren. They now live in Denver, Colorado.

"I will always remember my father's imperative to never give up."

MAGDA & IZAK SCHALOUM

RETIRED BUSINESS OWNERS
MAGDA: SURVIVOR OF AUSCHWITZ, PLASZOW, AND MÜHLDORF CONCENTRATION CAMPS
IZAK: SURVIVOR OF AUSCHWITZ-BIRKENAU, DACHAU, AND MÜHLDORF CONCENTRATION CAMPS

Tears well up quickly in Magda Schaloum's eyes when she recalls the final memories of her father. Through an open door of a train bound for Auschwitz, Magda, her brother, and her mother watched in horror as her father tried in vain to get a package of food to his family. At trackside, her father was brutally beaten by SS guards who then took the package and told him they would give it to his family. Instead, they kept it for themselves. Magda never saw her father again.

Magda, born Magda Altman, grew up in a well-to-do family in Felsogalla, Hungary. Her father was a successful locksmith. But as Hungary came under Nazi occupation in 1944, Magda, her brother, and her mother were forced to board a train bound for Auschwitz. After their arrival, they were separated. Magda's mother was sent to the gas chambers. She does not know her brother's fate.

After 10 days in the camp, Magda was sent to the Plaszow camp in Krakow. "This was the worst time. It was hot and exhausting. There was hard work, and the beatings. One day, the work foreman told us we could stop work and rest for a while. I was approached by an SS officer who asked why I was resting. Unable to speak his language, I could not reply. The SS officer beat me, while his dog was poised to attack me. The foreman, who witnessed the beating incident, slapped me, and assigned me the toughest labor for the remaining six-week period that I was at the camp."

In August 1944, Magda was sent back to Auschwitz, and in 1945, on to Augsburg, Germany, as a slave laborer in a factory. From there, she was sent to Mühldorf, a sub-camp of Dachau. That is where she met Izak, a Greek-born Jew who had been deported from Greece.

"To be human is to cherish and cultivate values in ourselves and our families."

Izak was born in 1918 in Saloniki, Greece. In 1942, he was sent in the second transport out of his town to Auschwitz-Birkenau, and there endured starvation and slave labor. He and his brother were then sent to Warsaw to clean up the destruction inflicted on the city by the Nazis. There, his skills as a leather tanner passed down by his father helped save his life. He was able to work in a factory in the concentration camp. However, they were then forced on a death march with other survivors to Dachau. As they marched, they went by a pond. The prisoners had nothing to eat or drink for many days, so many of the prisoners ran to the pond for a drink. Those who made it were immediately shot by the guards. Izak, one of the few survivors left, made it to Dachau and was then sent to Mühldorf.

At Mühldorf in April 1945, Izak and Magda saw each other for the first time. They were put on the same cattle wagon with other survivors to be transported to an unknown spot and murdered. Along the way, they were liberated by Allied troops. After liberation, they spoke to each other for the first time. She spoke only German and Hungarian and he only Greek. But, said Magda, he knew how to say, "I love you" and "Together, together."

The Schaloums immigrated to the United States after the war. They loved their freedom, but missed their families. They started a cleaning and laundry operation, and subsequently a surplus store. Today, their two sons have taken over the business and operate one of the largest surplus stores in the Northwest, in Seattle. Izak's health eventually failed, and he suffered a stroke in 1989. He passed away in early 1995.

PAUL SCHWARZBART

EDUCATOR, SPEAKER & HIDDEN CHILD OF THE HOLOCAUST

Looking out his window, Paul Schwarzbart could see the Austrian flag that was raised each day at the local school. He remembers the day it was replaced with the flag of the Third Reich. Without warning, the life of this five-year-old boy began to change.

Schwarzbart was born in 1933 to a longtime Viennese family whose roots in the city dated back to the 1700s. When the Nazi reign of terror began, the family fled. Their apartment was confiscated and given to non-Jews, their neighbors and playmates decorated their lapels with swastika buttons, and Paul's father, a worker at an import-export company, was fired from his job. Schwarzbart still has the letter from his father's company that said the firing was for political reasons and expressed the regret of the company to lose such a valued employee after so many years.

In the winter of 1938, the Schwarzbart family smuggled themselves into neutral Belgium to await exit visas to the United States. Just before the arrival of German troops, Belgian police arrested Schwarzbart's father for being an Austrian, and sent him to a labor camp in the Pyrenees mountains of France. Friedrich Schwarzbart documented his incarceration there in some 99 letters to his wife and son who were living in Brussels under strict Nazi rule. Schwarzbart's father later endured numerous concentration camps, and he was eventually murdered at Buchenwald in 1945, just two months before the camp's liberation.

Meanwhile, in the spring of 1943, young Paul's mother made a heart-wrenching decision to put her son under the care of the Jewish underground, who hid him at the Home Reine Elizabeth, a Catholic boys' school in the Ardennes near Luxembourg. There, for two years, he assumed the role of a Belgian Catholic under the name of Paul

"Each one of us can and should make a difference. Most Holocaust 'rescuers' made that decision as individuals and then acted upon it. To just stand by is to acquiesce."

Exsteen. The model student soon became an altar boy and Cub Scout leader and was secretly baptized. Unable to divulge his real identity, a painful loneliness gnawed at his heart. All the while, he wrestled with the agony and uncertainty of his parents' whereabouts.

Liberated by American troops in the fall of 1944, Schwarzbart made his way alone back to Brussels. He was 11 years old. On a crowded street, he and his mother, Sara, recognized one another and were reunited. They reapplied for visas to immigrate to the United States and finally, in 1949, they reached San Francisco. Paul graduated from the University of California at Berkeley, and was a high school teacher for 29 years.

In 1988, Schwarzbart discovered that the Home Reine Elizabeth where he hid during the war had been a secret haven for 86 other Jewish boys within the student body of 125. Indeed, he had not been the lone Jew hiding there during those years. Paul attended a reunion of these hidden children, who have since met again in New York and Brussels.

It was also in 1988 that Schwarzbart's dramatic story was told in an award-winning Ken Swartz documentary, *Shattered Dreams: A Child of the Holocaust,* which first aired on San Francisco television. The documentary shows how the reunion of the hidden children of "Jamoigne" was a milestone in all of the boys' lives.

Today, Paul Schwarzbart is professor of French and the director of the prestigious Maison Française, part of the University of California at Berkeley Extension Program. Paul and his late wife, Gail, have two sons, Marc and David. He volunteers countless hours to speak at high schools and colleges throughout California and Nevada about the Holocaust.

DAVID SCHWARZBERG

RETIRED CORPORATE FOREMAN & SURVIVOR OF THE KOZIENICE GHETTO
AND OF YELNO, RADOM, SKARZYSKO, AND BUCHENWALD CONCENTRATION CAMPS

David Schwarzberg's daughter was one of the first babies born of the generation that was not meant to be. Schwarzberg met his wife, Sara Cederboim, on a liberation train to the American zone of Germany. They were married in a Displaced Persons camp near Frankfurt a few months after the war's end, and, a year later, their daughter Peppy was born. Later, their children, Robert and Esther, were born in the United States. They are Schwarzberg's testimony to survival.

Schwarzberg was born in Kozienice, Poland, in 1924. He was 14 years old when Poland fell to Germany. He remembers the random killings and the cries of children being separated from mothers. The Nazis established a Jewish ghetto in Kozienice shortly after the war began. "They brought people into the ghetto from all around. My family had two rooms. They put another 16 or 18 people in with us. I said, 'This is the end.'" But for David, this was only the beginning. He was taken to the camps of Radom and Yelno and labored for two years. He returned to the ghetto at the end of 1942. Late that year, the ghetto was liquidated.

Schwarzberg was sent by truck to Skarzysko in Poland. There he worked moving steel used to make grenades. David was badly injured when a piece of steel fell on his foot. Often, an injury in the camp was a death sentence. Inmates not able to work were shot to death, but Schwarzberg survived. In an unusual twist, it was also at Skarzysko that Schwarzberg met officer Loeffler, an SS man who saved his life on more than one occasion. Loeffler provided David with extra bread for nearly two years. And when Schwarzberg was wrongly accused of stealing in the camp and was sentenced to be executed, Loeffler got him released and then moved him to a different area of the camp.

In 1944, Schwarzberg was transferred to Buchenwald. The end of the war neared, American bombs fell, and the inmates were taken to another camp. There, David worked in a factory as an engineer. Then, forced on a death march, they were sent back to Buchenwald and arrived on April 10. On April 11, 1945, the U.S. Army liberated the camp.

After the war, David searched for his family and found that two of his five siblings had survived, as well as three cousins who were in hiding near the Warsaw ghetto. He met his future wife, Sara, who is a survivor of Auschwitz. They married and had their first child while still in the Displaced Persons camp outside Frankfurt.

The Schwarzberg family was brought to New Jersey in 1950 by HIAS, the Hebrew Immigrant Aid Society. David worked at the Universal Manufacturing Corporation. They had two more children, Robert and Esther. Schwarzberg is now retired.

David's firstborn daughter, Peppy, is a Holocaust educator and works on the development and implementation of Holocaust curricula in New Jersey's public schools. In 1995, they returned together to Buchenwald to mark the 50th anniversary of Schwarzberg's liberation. This time, David was there as an honored guest.

"Auschwitz is not to understand. Auschwitz is to remember."

GERDA SEIFER

HOLOCAUST EDUCATOR AND COMMUNITY VOLUNTEER & HOLOCAUST SURVIVOR

For Gerda Seifer, light meant freedom. As a child during the Holocaust, she spent weeks in the dark, and years alone hiding from the Nazis, always fearing for her life.

The Germans marched into Seifer's hometown of Przemysl, Poland, in September of 1939, just two weeks after the start of World War II. Her father hid as the Nazis shot more than 200 Jewish men. Her mother kept the family business open and watched as the Nazis looted their store. By 1940, the family moved to a new city in Soviet-occupied territory, hoping to escape the Nazis and live in anonymity. The following year, Germany declared war on Russia, Nazis entered the city, and Jews were herded into a ghetto. Living in a house with 18 other families, there was little food, no supplies, and no way out.

Gerda remembers how the Germans descended on the ghetto with guns and dogs, shouting, ordering people out of the buildings. "Germans would shoot people on the spot if they were moving slowly, if they hesitated, or took time to pick up food or cover for their child. It was common for an SS man to kill a baby or child in front of its mother, or shoot a parent in front of a child. The ghetto looked like a war zone with blood on the streets, dead bodies everywhere, broken windows, and empty, eerie apartments with their doors left open. No one was coming back."

Before the Germans came again, Seifer's father asked a Catholic woman to hide his 15-year-old daughter in exchange for money. The woman agreed, hiding her in the potato cellar. She sat on a wooden box in total darkness for six weeks. "One day, when the cellar door was unlocked, I ran out on the street just to see the daylight, the sky, and the sun. It was August and the sky was very blue. I didn't care what would happen to me or who might see me. I just couldn't stand the darkness any longer," she said.

Seifer returned to the ghetto to find her family. She discovered her mother and cousin had been taken by the Nazis. Once again, her father arranged for her to be hidden. He had heard of a Catholic woman who needed help caring for her small children. The woman had had an illegitimate child who died in infancy, whose age would have corresponded with Gerda's. She went to live with the woman and became that child, Alicja Szumlanska. She was taught about Catholicism, went to church, and for more than three years, worked as an abused servant in her new "mother's" home. "I had to keep my private thoughts to myself, and I grieved for my real mother in silence," she remembers.

Using his work permit, her father stayed behind making whatever money he could to keep his daughter's identity and location a secret. One day, his payments and letters to his daughter ceased. Seifer later learned he had been turned in by a Pole and was arrested by the Nazis.

When the war ended, Gerda was 18. Nearly all of her 25 extended relatives had perished, and she had no place to go. She applied to leave Poland with a rabbi who was taking war orphans to England. Gerda was the last person to be added to his list.

Gerda Seifer started her new life in London, learned English, and trained as a nurse at St. James Hospital. In 1951, she immigrated to America and started her own family. She has served many Jewish and children's organizations as a volunteer. For more than 20 years, Seifer has toured schools, teaching students about the horrors of the Holocaust and the precious gift of freedom.

> "Freedom is a precious thing in America. We take it for granted. People must use their minds to determine what is wrong and right. Each individual must make his own choices."

NATHAN SHAPELL

COFOUNDER OF ONE OF THE NATION'S LARGEST HOMEBUILDERS, COMMUNITY LEADER, AUTHOR &
SURVIVOR OF AUSCHWITZ-BIRKENAU, GÜNTHERGRUBE, AND WALDENBURG CONCENTRATION CAMPS

For some, it was the Nazi atrocities against children that left the deepest scars. And for Nathan Shapell, it was the children's plight that made him want to survive and help.

Shapell was 17 when the Germans occupied his hometown of Sosnowiec in Poland. His father murdered and his family persecuted, Nathan used the only weapons he had to fight back: his ingenuity, his resourcefulness, and his courage.

When friends and family were deported, Nathan worked fervently to get them released. When his mother was "selected" for the Targowa ghetto, he used his position as a sanitation worker for the city to walk into Targowa with his broom and cart to bring her food. Shapell rescued many men from Targowa, disguising them as co-workers with official armbands of the sanitation department. But he wanted to save more lives. Nathan knew time was running out. No one knew when the Germans would make their next move.

On one trip into the ghetto, Shapell noticed large soup kettles that were brought in to feed the thousands of people packed into the ghetto's few square blocks. He devised a plan to hide three children, one child in each of the three soup kettles, and carry them out of the ghetto. "We did not know the children, nor they us. As in the case of the men, we rescued whoever was at hand. The children we brought out in those few days left an indelible mark on my life. Although they were strangers to me, their faces live forever in my memory. I have never forgotten, nor can I ever forget, their suffering."

Shapell's efforts to save people are documented in his book, *Witness to the Truth*. One of his most vivid memories is of a five-year-old girl.

"Now, as then, the face of an innocent child is my guiding light of hope for the world … the reason to survive, to achieve, and to work for the future."

"Like the rest, she dumbly accepted being placed in the greasy soup pot and made no sound as I carried her past the guards and into the street. When I set her down at the nearest safe corner, the child turned her face up to me and asked, 'Where shall I go?' I had to tell her, 'Child, I don't know. Run, run!'"

Nathan was eventually deported to Auschwitz-Birkenau, and survived two death marches and two more camps, Günthergrube and Waldenburg. At the war's end, 23 years old, his home destroyed, and most of his family dead, Shapell led a small group, including his only surviving sister, out of the Russian-occupied zone of Germany and into the American zone.

Determined not only to rebuild his own life, but to help others rebuild theirs, Shapell stayed in Europe for five years after the war, building a community for thousands of displaced people and survivors of the camps. Nathan immigrated to America in the early 1950s with his wife, Lilly, and young daughter. They later had a son.

In America, Nathan Shapell founded Shapell Industries, a highly successful real estate development company recognized as an industry leader and role model for corporate philanthropy. In addition to his business success, he has dedicated a great deal of his life to public service. Shapell has on the executive board of the American Academy of Achievement, as a member of President Reagan's Private Sector Survey on Cost Control, as well as on the Commission on California State Government Organization and Economy. He also founded Building a Better Los Angeles, an organization that helps the homeless, and has served as president of D.A.R.E. America, a renowned drug abuse resistance program that targets youth.

ABRAHAM SPIEGEL

INTERNATIONALLY KNOWN BUSINESSMAN, COMMUNITY LEADER, PHILANTHROPIST & SURVIVOR
OF AUSCHWITZ, FUNFTEICHEN, GROSS-ROSEN, AND BUCHENWALD CONCENTRATION CAMPS

There are four memorial candles flickering in 500 mirrors that reflect the light more than a millionfold. It is a stirring memorial to the 1.5 million children who were killed by the Nazis, including Uziel Spiegel, the son of Abraham and Edita Spiegel. Of all his accomplishments and successes, the memorial at Israel's Holocaust Museum is Abraham's most powerful and lasting contribution, for it was he who built this Children's Memorial at Yad Vashem.

Spiegel is from Munkacs, a small town in eastern Czechoslovakia, which today is part of the former Soviet Union. He was the fifth child in a family of nine. Their father, Haim Benjamin, was a religious Jew. He owned a sawmill and was both an astute businessman and a scholar. It was from his father that Abraham developed his love for Jewish studies and his business savvy. Spiegel studied in a yeshiva. He was president of the Hebrew library and study group of the first Hebrew college in Czechoslovakia before he joined the family business.

While on vacation, Spiegel met a woman from the city of Bardejov, Edita Rozenwasser. Because of the growing anti-Semitism and political tension, the two were married in a ceremony on the Czech-Hungarian border in order to allow both families to attend. It was November 1940.

Over the next four years, the family came under Nazi rule and persecution. In March 1944, Abraham, Edita, and their two-year-old son, Uziel, along with most of their extended family, were sent to Auschwitz. The men and women were separated from each other and either forced into slave labor or gassed.

Edita stood in front of Dr. Josef Mengele when she was separated from her mother and her baby son. Mengele, known to prisoners as the Angel of Death, conducted the camp selections, deciding who would live and who would die. Edita was told she would see her mother and child later, but she did not. They both were sent to the gas chambers.

Abraham endured the camps of Auschwitz, Funfteichen, Gross-Rosen, and Buchenwald. Toward the end of the war, he was among a group of 400 survivors from an original group of 6,000 sent on a death march to Sudetenland. He and others had overheard details of a Nazi plan to kill the prisoners. Spiegel suggested to the group that they escape. When the guard detail dropped from 40 to 5, the prisoners made a run for it. Spiegel and two other comrades encountered a young boy who was sympathetic to the escapees. They were sent to join the partisans 30 miles up the road and survived the war.

Russian forces took control of the area in May 1945. Spiegel and his wife were reunited. Their second son, Thomas, was born in 1946. They immigrated to the United States and eventually settled in California where their daughter Rita was born in 1948.

Spiegel began working in land development. He financed construction projects and built more than 10,000 houses for returning soldiers. By 1958, he had entered the banking business as well.

More than simply a builder of buildings, Abraham Spiegel has built institutions. In tribute to his young son and the 1.5 million other children killed in the Holocaust, he built the Children's Memorial at Yad Vashem. He founded the Nahum Goldmann Museum of the Jewish Diaspora in Tel Aviv. The Spiegels funded the establishment of the Spiegel Mathematics and Computer Building at Bar-Ilan University. They also established the Abraham & Edita Spiegel Chair in Holocaust Research, which has been vital in identifying and discrediting Holocaust revisionist theorists, and they created the "Uziel Garden" at the Bar-Ilan campus in memory of their son.

> *"We must teach our children and our children's children to guard our people, our lives, and our spirit, so that we cannot be destroyed like this ever again."*

MORRIS STEIMAN

RETIRED FURRIER & SURVIVOR OF THE GHETTO AND SEVERAL LABOR CAMPS

Morris Steiman remembers the beatings—beatings when they were herded into the ghetto, in the camps, and in the factories. "Although we were beaten down, knocked down, and degraded, we had the esteem to live," says Steiman.

Steiman is from Bodzanow, Poland, a small town with a Jewish population of 2,000 people. Still in his twenties, Morris and his family were driven from their homes in the spring of 1941. As they were herded toward the center of town, German trucks awaited them on one side of the street, and SS guards on the other.

"You had to pass by them in order to go to the center of town. I was with my father, mother, and others in my family. As people walked past the SS, they were beaten. When we passed, they hit my father on the head and he fell to the ground. A friend helped me pick him up, then I got hit on the head. Blood was coming out."

The Jews were loaded on trucks and taken to the city of Czestochowa where other Jews tended their wounds. Steiman met a young girl there whom he would marry in the ghetto two months later.

From Czestochowa, Morris and his new wife were sent to a number of camps and were slave laborers in ironworks and ammunition factories. "We were among the very few lucky people because we were able to be together during the whole war. We were together in the camps the whole time, not because I was smart; it was just one of those miracles that happened."

Steiman and his wife were working in an ammunition factory in Czestochowa. They worked day and night. Once Nazi guards beat his wife with a screwdriver for no apparent reason. Risking his own life,

"Dream the big dream. If you don't, no one will do it for you."

Steiman confronted the Nazi boss and pleaded, "'Beat me instead of my wife.' He could have shot me on the spot," says Morris. And Steiman was beaten in the factory many times. The prisoners in the factory had a saying: "Even if we finish our work today, they [the Nazis] will finish us tomorrow."

They worked as slave laborers from 1942 to the beginning of 1945 when the Russian Army liberated the camp. He remembers the last day in the camp when the prisoners did not know what was happening. They did not follow their usual work routine. The Nazi guard who was second in command at the camp had warned Steiman when the time came to stay in the barracks. That afternoon they heard artillery gunfire. "Around 7 p.m.," recalls Steiman, "the commander from the camp called us out and said, 'I was good to you, come with us.'" About 700 people did go and were apparently murdered. Steiman and his wife hid in the barracks. At about 10 p.m., they were freed. The following morning they went to the town of Czestochowa, where they were able to get food and clothing. "We were just beginning to find out what we lost: family, friends, towns, whole populations."

The Steimans stayed in Czestochowa until the end of 1945, then went to American-occupied West Germany. He contacted his sister in the United States and Steiman and his wife immigrated in 1947. The couple raised one daughter before Morris's wife died in 1968. He remarried in 1972.

Morris Steiman says he will always be thankful to God and the American country. He implores future generations to "learn from the experience. Nothing like this should ever happen again. Not to the Jewish people. Not to anybody in the world."

PAULA & KLAUS STERN

HOLOCAUST EDUCATORS – PAULA: SURVIVOR OF AUSCHWITZ CONCENTRATION CAMP
KLAUS: SURVIVOR OF AUSCHWITZ, SACHSENHAUSEN,
FLOSSENBÜRG, LEONBERG, AND MÜHLDORF CONCENTRATION CAMPS

Paula and Klaus Stern were newlyweds when the Gestapo deported them to a concentration camp. The young German couple worked on a farm owned by American Jews in Germany.

Klaus, a Berlin native, joined the farm to further his chances for emigration. Paula, formerly Paula Schaul, was working for the German forestry. They were married in 1942. "We figured it would be easier to get through the war being two."

For a time on the farm, the Sterns were safe from the ravages of war, though they could not keep any food they harvested for themselves. Everything was handed over to the Germans and the farm-workers went hungry.

In 1943, the Gestapo told the workers they had three days in which to train Ukrainians who would take over the farm. The Jewish youth were forced to sign documents that said they were spies against the German government. They were put in cattle cars destined for Auschwitz.

The Sterns were herded past a man they later learned was the infamous Dr. Josef Mengele, the Nazi doctor in charge of "selections" at Auschwitz. With a shake of his hand, he sorted those who would live from those who would die. "A woman in front of me had two small children," recalls Paula. "She was holding one, and I wanted to help her, so I took one child from her. Klaus yelled at me to give back the child. I did. That was my luck. If I had kept the child, I would have been in the row headed for the gas chambers."

Paula and Klaus were separated in the camp and for 28 months knew nothing of each other's fate. Paula worked in a munitions factory and was useful as the only German-speaking prisoner there. Klaus, meanwhile, dug trenches. He became known as a "musselman," or a walking skeleton. He lost 70 pounds and weighed only 95 pounds at the end of the war.

Klaus remembers the monthly "selections" in which the prisoners were forced to march naked in front of Nazi guards. "If you did not march fast enough, they would write down your number, and that would be the end of you. In 1944, I was down to nothing. I did not march fast enough and they wrote my number down. I knew it was the end of me." But each morning when he woke up, Klaus's face was swollen. That morning, they called his number, and those who had been "selected" were to be taken by truck to the gas chambers. There was a group of 75 to 100 people. Klaus was very tall. An SS guard saw him with his swollen face and said, "Hey, don't you know what group this is? Get out of the group! You look good enough to me to do a day's work."

Klaus was shipped from camp to camp and survived Auschwitz, Sachsenhausen, Flossenbürg, Leonberg, and Mühldorf. In the spring of 1945, Americans liberated the camps of both Paula and Klaus. Paula returned to her hometown where the couple agreed they would meet after the war. Klaus, sick with typhoid fever, wrote a letter that was handed from soldier to soldier through city after city. Six weeks later, Paula received it. The letter asked her to wait for him.

After their reunion, the Sterns immigrated to the United States. Klaus is a retired wholesale bakery employee. The couple raised two children, one of whom is now the executive director of the Pacific Northwest Region Anti-Defamation League of B'nai B'rith. Klaus remains active as a public speaker on the Holocaust.

> "We didn't survive to hate—but we hope that the world learned something from our experiences, so that atrocities like these will never happen again."

ISRAEL STUHL

INSURANCE ACCOUNTANT & SURVIVOR OF AUSCHWITZ-BIRKENAU,
AUSCHWITZ-BUNA, BUCHENWALD, AND THERESIENSTADT CONCENTRATION CAMPS

I live for tomorrow, not for the yesterdays," says Israel "Sruly" Stuhl. Israel's yesterdays include 12 months in four Nazi concentration camps and the deaths of 7 of his 10 family members.

Stuhl was 10 years old at the beginning of World War II. His family was from Slatinske Doly, in what was then Czechoslovakia. They lived under Hungarian rule in their hometown from 1939 to 1944. In May 1944 his family was deported to Auschwitz concentration camp. At age 15, the slender boy was an inmate at Auschwitz-Buna with the number A-6496. He feared, because of his slight build, that he would be mistaken for a weak prisoner and would be selected for extermination. Every six weeks, camp inmates had to walk naked in front of the camp doctors, including Dr. Mengele, known to the inmates as the Angel of Death. Mengele would make "selections," separating those who would live from those who would die.

Stuhl developed a sore on his leg that prevented him from working. Again he feared for his life. Following a brief treatment in the camp hospital, he quickly returned to the barracks to avoid being "selected."

After eight months in Auschwitz, Stuhl was sent, on foot, to Buchenwald. Prisoners were marched in the cold of January, without food or water, for three days and nights. They were then put on open railroad cars for a weeklong train trip. So many were shot and died en route. Stuhl remembers how "frozen bodies were thrown off the train unceremoniously."

From Buchenwald, Stuhl was transferred again, this time to Theresienstadt. There, he was liberated on May 8, 1945. He was hospitalized and regained his strength, only to contract tuberculosis in 1946. He recovered in a hospital in Germany.

Stuhl's father, Mechel Hersh Stuhl, his mother, Feiga Wollovitz Stuhl, four brothers, and a sister all died at Auschwitz. One brother and a sister survived. The three immigrated to the United States. Stuhl followed his siblings there in August 1950.

Israel Stuhl worked for many years as an accountant in the insurance industry and continues to work part time. His life is guided by the principle of "Tzedaka," or justice and righteousness. "I wish to be remembered by my patience, kindness, good deeds, and a love for all who are in need, notwithstanding my own experiences," he says. Despite the past, Stuhl says he lives, with patience and optimism, that tomorrow will bring a better world. After all, there remains in his heart hope eternal.

Stuhl and his wife raised two sons and they now have four grandchildren. He is an active member of his synagogue and a member of and contributor to many Jewish organizations and publications.

> *"Gentleness and humility are enormous human strengths awaiting discovery by mankind."*

HERMAN TAUBE

PRIZE-WINNING AUTHOR, POET, EDUCATOR, JOURNALIST, COMMUNITY LEADER, VOLUNTEER
AT THE U.S. HOLOCAUST MEMORIAL MUSEUM & SURVIVOR OF THE HOLOCAUST

Teaching and writing are my way of saying Kaddish, my yartzeit (memorial) candle for my lost people," writes Herman Taube. Taube has called himself a chronicler of his people's history. "I'm their memory, their recorder."

Taube is a native of Lodz, Poland. He was raised by his religious grandfather after the loss of his parents. He became a yeshiva student and a voracious reader of Polish and Yiddish books, old magazines, and his favorite—Friday supplements of the Yiddish newspaper *Der Nayer Folksblatt.*

Exiled from his home by war, Herman left behind his world of study to become a medic. He worked in an army lazaret and first-aid station, ministering to the suffering Jewish and gentile refugees. All the while, Taube kept writing. "After being wounded, I used the power of writing to revive my memory. There were not only black and blue marks on my body but dark and shadowy conflicts in my mind … mingling all of them with the stories of people I met, the tales that fascinated me helped me remember …"

Taube served in the Second Polish Army and was stationed in Majdanek. He participated in the liberation of Poland and administered medical care to those who survived the camps. Of seeing the liberated camp, Herman writes, "My voice was choked and my tongue stifled when I saw Majdanek. The only things that continued were the flow of tears and the nightmares."

Herman's wife, Susan, is a survivor of the Riga ghetto and Kaiserwald and Stutthof concentration camps. Both their families perished in the Holocaust. Today, they have five children and 10 grandchildren.

Herman Taube came to America in 1947. Since that time, he has been writing for the Yiddish *Forward* and formerly penned a column for the *Washington Jewish Week.* At 65, he completed a master's degree in literature and creative writing from American University. Over the years, he has taught high school and college, and has lectured widely.

> *"We can build a future only if we remain loyal to our traditions and have reverence for our past. Bearing witness to our past gives us meaning to our present and a renewed sense of values for our children for the future."*

He is the author of 17 volumes of poetry and novels. His writings include *Land of Blue Skies, Kyzyl Kishlak: Refugee Village, Autumn Travels, Devious Paths, My Baltimore Landsmen,* and *Between the Shadows.* In the latter, the author is standing before a monument in Warsaw, and he hears the stones talking to each other, telling the horror stories of Jewish martyrdom, of desperate resistance, and of the heroism of the Jewish youth in the ghetto uprising. Taube hides one of the "live" stones, and brings it home:

I keep him in our
china closet, with my
Sabbath Kaddish cup,
candlesticks, and
Havdalah (candle) holder.
Often, when the house
is asleep and visions
burn my mind
I take the stone
into my hands;
like friends,
we share our secret memories.
The stone has a heart.
Inside it vibrates
a battery and a tape
which plays repeatedly
Remember! Remember!
Four hundred thousand
martyrs of Warsaw Ghetto!
Sometimes, past midnight,
I think I hear the stone cry:
Why? Why? Why?
I take the stone
hold it to my face
and wash it with my tears.

Taube says his poems are simple, easy to read, but difficult to enjoy. They are, he says, personal notes—outpourings of images and emotions dealing with pain, nightmares, war, poverty—and a lament, an outcry of one individual against society. "I'm possessed by a Dibbuk, a spirit who constantly pushes paper and pencil into my hands and forces me to write. A voice in my brain calls, 'Keep recording! You are the voice of a lost generation.'"

NECHAMA TEC

UNIVERSITY PROFESSOR, SCHOLAR, PRIZE-WINNING AUTHOR, LECTURER & SURVIVOR OF THE HOLOCAUST

Nechama Tec, a writer and a professor of sociology at the University of Connecticut, is a scholar of the Holocaust. She has recently been appointed as Senior Research Fellow at the U.S. Holocaust Memorial Museum in Washington, D.C.

Four of her six books probe deeply into that hour of history. For the last 20 years, she has been documenting the fate of European Jewry. Nechama's research and publications focus on compassion, mutual help, altruism, rescue, resistance to evil, courage, and survival. Rare and easily overshadowed by the enormity of the German crimes, these special features contributed to Jewish survival.

Nechama was eight years old when the Germans invaded her hometown, Lublin, Poland. After a stay in the ghetto, she and her family moved illegally to the forbidden Christian world, taking refuge with Christian Poles. For almost three years, her parents never left their apartment, while she and her sister, living under assumed names, were pretending to be Catholics.

Following the war, Nechama resumed her Jewish identity and for the last two decades has written and lectured in the United States and abroad about the destruction of European Jews. Each of Nechama's books has gained recognition and awards. In 1995, *Defiance: The Bielski Partisans* received the first prize for Holocaust Literature in Israel from the World Federation of Fighters, Partisans, and Ghetto Inmates, and in 1994 it was awarded the International Anne Frank, Special Recognition Prize. Her book, *In the Lion's Den: The Life of Oswald Rufeisen,* was nominated for a Pulitzer Prize and received the 1991 Christopher Award. In the following quotation from her autobiography, *Dry Tears,* Nechama offers a glimpse of her life while passing as a Catholic:

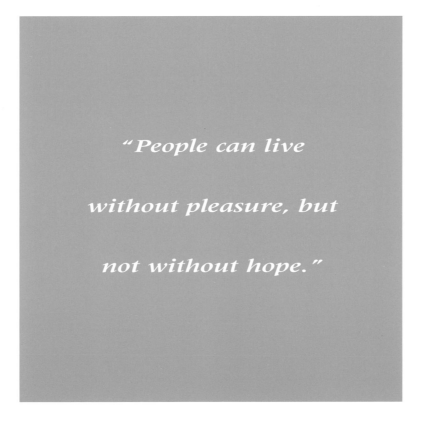

"People can live

without pleasure, but

not without hope."

Janka was a friend to whom I felt especially close. One evening, she began telling me a story that had to do with Jews catching Christian children, murdering them, and using their blood for matzoh. At first I listened impassively, but then a strong urge came over me to correct her distorted view.

I was convinced that if she really knew the facts she would certainly change her way of thinking and talking about the Jews. As innocently as I could, I asked, "Do you really believe Jews do that? Have you seen it happen?" I could see that she was startled, there was a long silence. Then she turned to me and said angrily, "How strange, Krysia, that you should ask such a thing. Everybody knows Jews do that, but they're smart, they do it secretly! So how could I have seen such a thing?"

As she scrutinized me in anger and disbelief, my heart sank. What if she suspected me? I was really scared, too scared to say anything, and my heart pounded heavily through another oppressive silence. Then, with a slightly changed tone, Janka said, "You're still a baby, young and dumb, that is what you are!"

I was relieved, but for days I had terrible fantasies about her denouncing me, and I blamed myself for destroying all of us. Too ashamed and frightened to report this episode to my parents, I waited all alone, in constant agony, convinced that each day would be our last. The anticipated disaster did not happen, but I had learned my lesson. I tried harder than ever not to make any comments at all about Jews, and did not disagree with anything derogatory that was said about them.

Placed within the devastating environment of the Holocaust, Nechama's books are permeated with hope. She feels that "it is important for children to know that even in the dark times of the Holocaust some Christians and Jews risked their lives to save the persecuted and helpless Jews."

MICHAEL THALER, M.D.

PROFESSOR OF PEDIATRICS, SCIENTIST, HISTORIAN, AUTHOR, FORMER PRESIDENT OF THE HOLOCAUST CENTER OF NORTHERN CALIFORNIA & SURVIVOR OF THE BRZEZANY GHETTO

Four days after Michael Thaler and his mother escaped from the ghetto, the 400-year-old Jewish community of Brzezany ceased to exist. He remembers the morning of June 12, 1943, when shots, shouts, and screams, then bursts of machine-gun fire, signaled the beginning of the final massacre. He peered between the loose planks of a barn loft as the remaining 2,500 Jews of Brzezany were slaughtered.

The barn belonged to former neighbors, an elderly Polish couple who, in 1942, hid the eight-year-old Michael, while the rest of his family endured life inside the ghetto walls. "The gaunt figure of my father appeared on a snowy night in mid-March 1943. He had come at the risk of his life to take me back to the ghetto. Other Jewish children in hiding and their gentile rescuers had been betrayed by collaborators and hanged. Several weeks after my return, we were held as hostages and marked for execution should the community fail to satisfy the latest demands of the Gestapo for money, gold, and gems. A friend of the family stuffed me into a garbage can, which he carried to the rear of the building. He then dragged me, still in the can, through the empty night streets to his workplace in the former courthouse."

Thaler hid in a crawl space of the old stone building. As he peeked through a grated vent, he could see the courtyard of the jail where the Gestapo were beating people—people he recognized as fellow prisoners from the night before. A selection was in progress. "I was still trying mightily to identify my parents when the stack (of boxes) on which I stood collapsed and a hand was immediately clasped over my mouth. Wordlessly, the man who had brought me here carried me through a subterranean labyrinth to a door that led to the outside. 'Run!' he said, and pointed toward the ghetto." Michael returned to the ghetto to find his mother, who had been released. His father and other relatives were on their way to the slave labor camp of Kamionka.

As the ghetto roundups continued, Michael and his mother once again sought refuge with the Polish couple. His father escaped the labor camp, and on the slim chance of finding his family, returned to their refuge at the barn. After the destruction of the ghetto, Michael and his parents were forced to flee to the forest to avoid being captured during a house-to-house search. They later returned to the barn and hid there for nearly a year until the Red Army reclaimed Brzezany in July 1944. When the war ended in May 1945, the Thaler family found themselves in a Displaced Persons camp near Linz, Austria, where they remained for three years.

The Thalers immigrated to Canada in 1948. Michael attended high school, college, and medical school in Toronto. He married and, with his wife, raised two children. He is a professor of pediatrics at the University of California in San Francisco. He is the author of 170 original scientific and clinical publications, and has been honored with numerous awards for public service. He served as president of the Holocaust Center of Northern California for 11 years.

Dr. Thaler says the most vital historic treasure to be salvaged from the Holocaust is the epic story of the victims' lives. "It was a half century ago, but the world is just beginning to confront the true dimensions of what happened," he says.

> *"Begin building the scholarly institutes needed to explore, record, and transmit to our children the awe-inspiring achievements of the Jewish people, the true target of Nazi dementia."*

WILLIAM UNGAR

BUSINESS LEADER, ENTREPRENEUR, PHILANTHROPIST &
SURVIVOR OF THE JANOWSKA CONCENTRATION CAMP

William Ungar came to America after World War II on the first ship carrying concentration camp survivors. The SS *Marine Flasher* reached the United States on May 20, 1946. Each of the refugees onboard was given $15 by the Jewish Joint Distribution Committee, a gesture Ungar later was to return a thousandfold with humanitarian deeds.

Before the war, William was a teacher at a technical high school in Lvov, Poland. One of his students gave Ungar his Polish identification papers, which allowed Ungar to pose as a non-Jew and to escape the Nazi atrocities.

Later, William was betrayed by someone unknown to him, was arrested by the Gestapo, and was interned in the Janowska concentration camp in Lvov. From there, he miraculously escaped and returned to the building where he resided prior to the outbreak of the war. The Ukrainian building superintendent, with whom he was friendly, agreed to hide him in the basement, despite the knowledge that the building was then occupied by the Gestapo and their families.

After the war ended, Ungar went to a displaced persons (DP) camp in Berlin and there received a visa to the United States. He arrived in New York City and made his home there. With his experience in a Polish technical high school, William found a job with a company that manufactured machinery that produced envelopes. He attended evening classes at the City College of New York and graduated as a mechanical engineer.

After five years at the machinery factory, Ungar decided to establish an envelope manufacturing business for himself. In 1952, the New York Envelope Corporation was born. It occupied 1,600 square feet with three full-time and two part-time employees, producing 200,000 envelopes per day. Today, under the banner of the National Envelope Corporation, the largest privately owned envelope company in the nation employs 2,500 people, with nine manufacturing facilities in eight states, and produces 90 million envelopes daily.

Like most Holocaust survivors, Ungar constantly wrestles with the imponderable question: "Why did I survive and others didn't? Why was I only wounded and others were killed? I survived to be a witness to what took place. And I also think God let me live to see what good I would do. This may be a very primitive way to answer the question but I feel that if I did survive, it was to do some good deeds in my lifetime."

Today, Ungar's return on "human investments" has earned him and his company numerous accolades from within the industry and the general business community as well for his "vision and innovation."

William says his Holocaust experience influences the way he conducts his business. "I believe that the human element in this changing world is the key to success. Our focus is to cultivate high moral standards, proper work ethics, and a spirit of harmony. We treat our staff with respect and dignity and they respond with loyalty." The Holocaust experience also imbued his longtime commitment to philanthropic efforts. Whether it is contributing to worthy causes or loaning his loyal employees interest-free money to buy a home, Ungar says his acts of kindness are repayment to his fellowman for the kindness that saved his life during the war.

William Ungar is married and has four daughters and 17 grandchildren. They, says Ungar, are his crowning achievement.

> *"This blessed country offers tremendous opportunities to any individual. With hard work and perseverance, one may hopefully achieve and fulfill his dreams."*

SOLOMON URBACH

RETIRED BUILDER AND JEWISH COMMUNITY LEADER & SURVIVOR OF THE KRAKOW GHETTO, PLASZOW AND GROSS-ROSEN CONCENTRATION CAMPS, AND A SCHINDLER JEW

The night of March 12, 1943, factory owner Oskar Schindler told his Jewish workers they could not go home because there was trouble. Home was the Krakow ghetto and Schindler knew that the Nazis planned to liquidate the ghetto that night. Solomon Urbach was 15. While he slept in Schindler's enamelware factory, his parents and five brothers and sisters were either deported to Auschwitz and gassed or killed during the brutal liquidation.

Urbach was one of the first 100 Jews who went to work in Schindler's factories. The German Catholic industrialist employed the workers and saved them from the fate that befell 6 million others. Schindler is credited with saving 1,300 Jews during the war.

Solomon remembers how, in 1942, four SS guards rounded up 100 Jews off the streets in the Krakow ghetto and put them into two trucks. "We were delivered to the Emalia factory. There was no explanation. When we got to the factory a tall civilian came out to inspect us. We did not know it, but we were to become the work force for this civilian, Oskar Schindler."

Solomon Urbach was the son of a tailor. The family lived in Krakow where Solomon attended public and religious school. With the start of World War II, Jews were banned from the schools and Urbach's family was forced into hiding.

In 1941, the Urbachs and 50,000 other Jews of Krakow were forced into a 20-by-20-block area of the Krakow ghetto. "We spent our days looking for food and trying to avoid the roundups that sent our brethren to forced labor and concentration camps. The roundup that finally gathered me ultimately saved my life."

Urbach worked for Schindler as a carpenter, fixing cabinets and doors in the enamelware factory that produced pots and pans. Solomon's main responsibility was to maintain the blackout shades, window shades pulled down during bombing attacks.

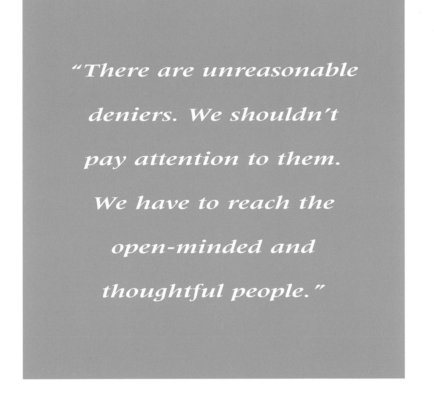

"There are unreasonable deniers. We shouldn't pay attention to them. We have to reach the open-minded and thoughtful people."

Urbach remained a Schindler "employee" from 1942 to 1945, with periodic transfers to other concentration camps. He was interned twice at Plaszow, a camp known for its brutal treatment of prisoners. Whenever a new Nazi order would ship his workers to a concentration camp, Schindler would bribe or bargain their way back to safety.

In the autumn of 1944, Schindler was ordered to reduce his work force from 1,000 to 300. "We were lined up. SS guards and their dogs helped Schindler in the selection. We had no way of knowing what fate was to befall either of the two groups being formed. Responding to an inner sense and gut feeling, I risked everything by stepping out of formation to directly address Oskar Schindler. 'Herr Schindler,' I shouted, 'Kein tischler ist geblieben!' (Mr. Schindler, no carpenter is left!) Schindler recognized me and placed me in the group of 300 that stayed in the factory."

Solomon was later sent to Gross-Rosen concentration camp. Once again, he was selected with a group of other prisoners, and packed into cattle cars headed for Brünnlitz, Czechoslovakia, where Schindler set up his last wartime factory. The Jews were liberated on May 8, 1945, by the Russians. Urbach set out on foot for Krakow to search for his family. He found no one. He immigrated to America in 1949 and married Ada Birnbaum, also from Krakow, who survived the war in a Siberian work camp.

Solomon Urbach founded a successful construction company. He and his wife raised three children and now have five grandchildren. For 25 years, he has been chairman of the Israel Bond Committee to help fund capital projects in Israel and aid in the resettlement of displaced Jews. He speaks about the Holocaust at universities, churches, synagogues, and schools, and says he has confidence that today's youth will understand the dangers and tragedies of hatred.

DORIS & FELIX URMAN

DORIS: MOTHER, GRANDMOTHER & SURVIVOR OF A SIBERIAN LABOR CAMP
FELIX: SURVIVOR OF THE LIQUIDATION OF KRESHOV AND A HIDDEN JEW

They live for and through their children. Doris and Felix Urman are Polish Jews and each survived the Holocaust. The families they have created in America are their declaration of survival and their piece of eternity in a fragile world.

"I always tried to provide my children with a home rich in tradition and values. I taught my children to respect others. They are my pride and joy and a symbol of my survival. Love is what sustains me," writes Doris.

Doris is from the town of Tomaszow Lubelski. She and her family were interned in a Soviet labor camp in Siberia from 1940 to 1942. Her grandfather, father, brother, sister, and a small group of devoted friends were together in the camp, facing starvation and working long hours in frigid temperatures with little clothing or protection. It was here that her grandfather died of starvation. "For me, the lowest point was after we were free and we returned to Poland to find that there was no one left, no family or friends to whom to say, look at what happened to us."

Doris immigrated to America in 1950, the same year as Felix. Each married a survivor and raised two children, and each lost a spouse. Felix's wife passed away in 1971. Doris's husband was murdered in New York in 1969—a victim of a mugging in Brooklyn. Doris and Felix married in 1972.

Felix had lost his entire family of nine in the war. They were killed in 1942 when the Germans exterminated the population of his hometown of Kreshov, Poland. Felix was a tailor, and, at his mother's insistence, took a job in the town at the local German headquarters repairing German uniforms. "After murdering all the Jews in the town, the soldiers returned to the headquarters to shoot me and the other two Jews working there, but we ran when we heard all the gunfire."

For the remaining two years of the war, Felix was hidden in a hayloft by a Polish Christian farmer. "I was hiding in the loft on a mat of hay, living amid the smells and sounds of the barn animals. The farmer who was hiding me, a man who had known my father and had bartered farm produce for tailoring, would discreetly pass me food in a bucket suspended from the loft, but only when he was certain that no one could see him. And when he was certain that there was absolutely

no one around, under cover of night, I would come down from the loft for a few minutes to move my legs. I never went outside the barn.

"At times, I did not really want to live knowing that everyone I knew and loved was dead. But my mother had begged me to do whatever I could to save myself so that some remnant of our family might survive. I lived, I persisted in this dark time in order to honor my mother's wish and her memory."

The families the Urmans lost are also honored with the Urmans' new family. Between them, Doris and Felix have eight grandchildren. Now, says Felix, "I'm the richest man in the world with children and grandchildren to love."

Doris's daughter is actively involved in the creation of the A Living Memorial to the Holocaust-Museum of Jewish Heritage in New York City, a museum designed to bring to life the richness and tradition of the vibrant communities annihilated in the Holocaust.

"Never allow your past or your sorrows to affect your ability to live and love in the present and to create a better future."

JACK WELNER

CARPENTER, HOLOCAUST EDUCATOR & SURVIVOR OF THE LODZ GHETTO AND AUSCHWITZ-BIRKENAU, KAUFERING-DACHAU, UTTING AT AMMERSEE-DACHAU, AND DACHAU CONCENTRATION CAMPS

As Jack Welner was pulled away from his mother at Auschwitz, she placed a piece of bread in his hand, saying, "You take it, you'll need it." It was the last time he saw her.

They had been deported to Auschwitz from the Lodz ghetto in Poland. There, they had lived in the ghetto for more than four years. Welner then survived four more concentration camps during the last 10 months of World War II.

He was born Jacob Nuta Welniarz in Lodz, Poland. He was one of five children of Joshua and Esther Welniarz. His father died when he was 10 years old. At the age of 19, he and the rest of his family were herded into the ghetto.

Welner worked in a lumber mill in the ghetto. Using a table saw, he removed the bark from tree logs that were then cut into boards and used to make shower slippers for the German Army.

Jack recalls the years in the ghetto when the only topic of conversation was food and when hunger, starvation, and hopelessness filled his family's lives. In 1942, his sister, Henia, and her seven-year-old son were taken away in one of the German roundups. In June 1944, his older brother, Shmulek, died of starvation. Then, in August 1944, Welner, his mother, and youngest sister, Chana, were deported to Auschwitz. Before getting into the cattle car that would take them there, the Germans gave each prisoner a piece of bread. Welner and his sister ate their bread immediately. Their mother kept her piece untouched. That was the bread she gave him once they reached the death camp.

After a week in Auschwitz, Welner and 70 other prisoners were transferred to Kaufering, a quarantine camp of Dachau. From there, Jack was sent to a labor camp, Utting-Ammersee, where he stayed until the spring of 1945. He worked in the camp at an iron-bending machine, and his German boss took a liking to him. His boss brought scraps of food to him and gave him an outdated newspaper that Welner turned in for an extra bowl of soup.

The camp was liquidated in late April 1945 and all the prisoners were taken to Dachau. The following day they were led on a death march south toward the Alps. Prisoners who could no longer march dropped to the ground and were shot by SS guards. The prisoners were liberated by the U.S. Army on May 2, 1945.

After the war, Welner entered a hospital. When he was strong enough to walk again, Jack obtained food from an American military kitchen and took it to his former boss, Hans Stefan, whose address had been forwarded to him by fellow inmates. Welner credits Stefan with saving his life.

> *"Integrity, honor, and honesty are characteristics of righteous human beings. These characteristics transcend all ethnic, social and economic boundaries"*

In the summer of 1945, Welner returned to Poland in search of survivors. In Lodz, he found one sister alive. He traveled for a month to Bergen-Belsen where he had heard that another sister had survived. Welner remained in Europe until February 1950, when he immigrated to America.

Jack Welner joined relatives in Denver, Colorado, married, and, after his wife's death, raised three children alone. He is a retired carpenter and devotes his time to speaking in schools about his Holocaust experience. Most of all, he says, he enjoys his time with his children and grandchildren.

ALEXANDER WHITE

THEATER PRODUCER, DIRECTOR & PARTISAN FIGHTER AND SURVIVOR OF A SERBIAN CONCENTRATION CAMP

Alexander White came to America alone as a 17-year-old refugee. His mother, father, two sisters, and a brother were murdered at Auschwitz.

White, born Sandor Weisz, grew up on his family's farm in Beregszasz on the border between Czechoslovakia and Hungary. As a young teen, he went to Budapest and studied at the Budapest Academy of Dramatic Arts. Alexander went to a movie house one evening and was arrested by the Gestapo for violation of the 5:30 p.m. curfew for Jews. He was put in a cattle car and sent to a Serbian concentration camp to work in an underground copper mine.

After eight days in the camp, White escaped and joined the partisan fighters loyal to Yugoslav guerilla leader Marshal Tito. He was a partisan fighter until the end of the war. He then returned home where he discovered his family had been sent to Auschwitz and gassed.

Tired of fighting, Alexander wanted to leave Europe. He immigrated to America with the help of the United Nations and the Joint Distribution Committee. He became a citizen and worked as a salesman. In Cleveland, Ohio, White had the chance to meet a New York theater producer, also a Hungarian. After they became good friends, White decided to make the theater his life's endeavor.

From 1948 to 1950, White studied at the Goodman Theatre School in Chicago. He went from working as a stage manager to directing and producing numerous theater productions. Alexander has worked as a director all over the United States, including with the New York Theater Production Company, the Los Angeles Repertory Theater, and the Cincinnati Playhouse. His directing credits include working with stars such as Judy Holiday, Geraldine Page, and Carroll O'Connor.

By age 28, White started a tent arena theater in Indianapolis. He opened with *Tonight or Never.* "Alexander White, the director-producer who promised to establish and maintain a high standard right from the start is a man of his word," said one newspaper account. The following year, he started a summer professional repertory theater-in-the-round in Cincinnati. Of White's production of *The Rainmaker* at the Cincinnati Summer Playhouse one critic wrote: "The only unfortunate thing is that it sets such a high standard that the plays yet to come will have to be whoppers to compare with it."

White says that in the theater, he has found a creative channel of expression that for years rested in the darkness of oppression. His dreams long obscured now dance in the light of the theater stage.

Today, Alexander White is married and has four children and four grandchildren. He encourages tolerance and kindness for one's fellowman. "People are all the same. We cry. We laugh. We live. I hurt as much as the next man. I bleed as much. I live the best life I can."

"Let us embrace life together and pursue life's abundance."

ABRAHAM ZUCKERMAN

REAL ESTATE DEVELOPER, AUTHOR, FOUNDING MEMBER OF THE U.S. HOLOCAUST
MEMORIAL MUSEUM & SURVIVOR OF THE PLASZOW, MAUTHAUSEN,
AND GUSEN II CONCENTRATION CAMPS AND A MEMBER OF SCHINDLER'S LIST

Abraham Zuckerman and his family lived in the Jewish section of Krakow known as Kazimierz. It took its name from Casimir the Great of Poland, who, in the fourteenth century, invited the Jews to Poland to take part in commerce and trade. With the start of World War II, however, Jews were afraid to be seen on the streets.

"Immediately after the Nazi occupation, my father and I hid in the attic in the apartment building where we lived. I remember that I used to stay in the attic and look through the round windows up there. I remember how the Nazis grabbed people and put them on their open green trucks. I can still see the trucks filled with people and God knows what happened to them."

Zuckerman was 14 when he and his family fled Krakow and eventually settled in Dukla. In 1941, the Nazis ordered all Jews to assemble in the Dukla church square. The community leaders were taken behind the church and shot. All but the young men were loaded onto trucks and taken away—most likely to Auschwitz. "I remember I wanted to go on the truck with my family. My mother pushed me away. She insisted that I stay with the other young men. The trucks left; that was the last time I saw my mother, father, or sisters alive."

Abraham ended up in the Plaszow concentration camp. He was there for several months when he was chosen to work in a factory run by a Catholic, Oskar Schindler. Schindler is the German industrialist who sheltered Zuckerman and more than 1,300 other Jews by employing them in his enamelware factory.

In 1944, Schindler's work force was cut in half. Nazis loaded hundreds of Schindler's workers, including Zuckerman, into railroad cars. "When the railroad cars were filled, the Nazis moved them to a side track. It was the middle of the summer and the heat was unbearable. We were not fed. We were given no water. After a couple days, I looked through the window in the railroad car and I saw Herr Schindler. He issued an order for the cars to be sprayed with cold water to cool them."

They were taken to Mauthausen and then to Gusen II where Zuckerman worked on an assembly line manufacturing V-2 rockets and fighter planes. Abraham was liberated from Gusen on May 5, 1945, and said he would never have survived the brutality and starvation in the camps were it not for the care he received from Schindler.

Later, Zuckerman spent four years in a displaced persons camp in Bindermichl, Austria, where he met his wife, Millie. She, too, survived the Holocaust with her family by hiding in an attic for two years. The couple married and immigrated to America in 1949. The Zuckermans have raised three children and now have eight grandchildren.

Zuckerman became a successful real estate developer in New Jersey. "The first thing we did in every development," Zuckerman says, "was to name a street after Oskar Schindler." There are now more than 25 Schindler streets and drives in New Jersey.

Abraham Zuckerman also remains committed to Jewish education and remembrance of the Holocaust. Author of *A Voice in the Chorus,* Zuckerman was honored with a Doctor of Law degree from the Rabbinical College of America and an honorary doctorate from Kean College. He holds positions on the boards of the American Gathering of Jewish Holocaust Survivors and the Great Synagogue of Jerusalem, and is a founding member of both the Simon Wiesenthal Center in Los Angeles and the U.S. Holocaust Memorial Museum in Washington, D.C.

Zuckerman is always mindful of a passage from Deuteronomy: "Only guard yourself, and guard your soul carefully, lest you forget the things your eyes saw, and lest these things depart your heart, all the days of your life. And you shall make them known to your children and to your children's children."

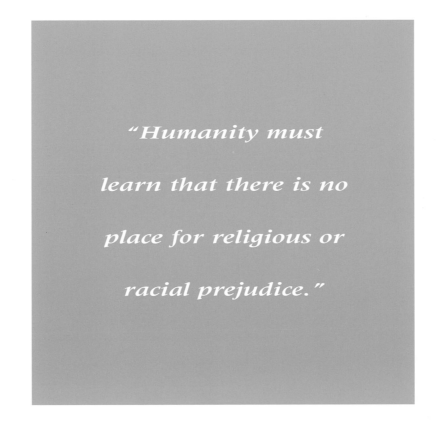

"Humanity must learn that there is no place for religious or racial prejudice."

AFTERWORD

In November 1991, I embarked on a month-long journey to create portraits of my extended family in Italy and other relatives who had replanted their post–World War II roots in Belgium and France. My flight from Denver terminated in Frankfurt, but I chose instead to head by train to Munich to spend the night. While en route, I was scanning a map of the region when my eyes locked on to the name of a village that had last pierced my consciousness as a high school student.

It was Dachau.

Could it be, I wondered, "that place" that I had heard, read, and studied about as a student? Suddenly, a strong pull overcame me and I elected to spend the night in that quiet, peaceful village. I had to experience Dachau, the infamous death camp. It was the site and symbol of Nazi terrorism and bestiality where thousands of Jews were killed because they were "different." As a teenager, I was unable to understand why the Nazis adopted a calculated strategy to annihilate all Jews. I studied extensively the Nuremberg War Crimes trials. While doing so, I discovered to my astonishment the systematic process that the Nazis devised to slaughter, gas, burn, starve, and work their Jewish captives to death. All because they were "different."

That singular day's visit was later to alter the course of my life over the next several years, and it forged a bold vision for my photographic talents. As a journalist, I was compelled to document the Jews who had exited alive from Dachau and other killing camps, and to document that they did, indeed, "triumph over Hitler," and are now living symbols of hope and compassion for all mankind.

During the subsequent five-year process, nearly every one of the 145 Survivors who appeared before my lens expressed curiosity about the answers to two questions: "Why are you doing this?" and "Are you Jewish?"

So, why did I, a non-Jew, undertake this project?

I told them that the day will come when the last Holocaust witness will perish and that final voice will be silenced forever. For overwhelming humanitarian reasons, I was moved to document their faces and their stories so the world may be informed by an impartial observer. Then and now, I am truly astonished to hear reports that the world was choosing to either forget or even deny that the Holocaust ever happened.

Today, these Holocaust Survivors are dramatic, living symbols of what is happening and can happen to other ethnic groups who are "different" and unacceptable to those who are fueled by hate. Humanity still has not learned the lesson from the Holocaust. One has only to read today's headlines and see the horrific scenes of partially decomposed bodies in mass graves in Bosnia. Hate and a bestial desire to conduct ethnic cleansing are very much alive half a century after the Holocaust.

Also, as a non-Jew, I sought to provide positive and uplifting messages of hope for humanity from an unlikely group of people who had every reason not to have hope. These Holocaust Survivors cherish their freedom and do not take it for granted. Their stories and messages to future generations inspire and rekindle hope that everyone can live a more productive life. Perhaps these stories and messages will resonate for those who may have abandoned all hope, such as growing numbers of today's youth who may be leading destructive lives. Many of the Survivors herein are glowing metaphors for what an individual can achieve when one is determined to give wings to one's own life's dream.

ACKNOWLEDGEMENTS

I wish to acknowledge a very special group of Holocaust survivors who opened both their homes and their hearts. Because of them, this book will also speak for those thousands of diminishing numbers who are unable to be represented in these pages. There were numerous moments when we laughed together and wept together, out of sadness or out of pure joy. They are now part of my life.

There are many individuals who offered counsel, encouragement, and their special talents so *The Triumphant Spirit* would take flight and enable me to create a national exhibition, publish this book, and produce a CD-ROM.

Primary among them is Nancy Dick, a valued friend who always offered reasoned counsel. Others whose talents and gifts enriched the experience and the final product are: Saul Rosenthal, for his solid direction and seasoned perspective; Thomas Keneally, whose stature in the literary world enhanced the meaning of the message; Dr. Jan Karski, who is revered by those who value humility and compassion; Rich Clarkson, whose influence was ever present during the photographic and publishing process; Leopold (Pfefferberg) Page, a newfound friend whose support never wavered and who generously offered his spirited assistance; Carrie Jordan, whose elegant design framed the stories and the portraits with striking visual integrity, equal to the measure of the historical content; Drew Myron, for the heart-and-soul quality of her writing contributions; Renee Rockford, for her lucid portrayals that seem to come to life on the page; Bernard R. Lange, who crafted the prints within these pages; Bruce Marsden, my assistant, who contributed unselfishly of his time, talent, and skills to assure that others would be influenced positively.

There are many who deserve my gratitude and acknowledgement for their wisdom, assistance, and loyalty at various times and in various ways. They are: Steven B. Cohen, Rusty Pallas, Linda Tafoya, Kathy Bauer & Jim Stouffer, Hilary & Charles St. John, Skip Kohloff, Peter Nagel, Emmerich Oross, Caryl Riedel, Lori Kranz, Tony Campbell, Rhode L. Chase, John Coombe, Emil Gold, Ernest Michel, Abe & Ann Oster, Sally Levenstein, Murray Pantirer, Abraham Zuckerman, Michael Green, Rae Kushner, Fanya Gottesfeld Heller, Angie & Moritz Goldfeier, Dr. Alex Grobman of the Martyrs Memorial & Museum of the Holocaust in L.A., Mary Song and Henry Friedman of the Washington State Holocaust Education Resource Center in Seattle, Lani Silver & John Grant of the Holocaust Oral History Project in San Francisco, Stanlee Stahl of the Jewish Foundation for Christian Rescuers in New York, and Peppy Margolis of the Holocaust Education & Remembrance Council of MetroWest.

Special gratitude is extended to: The Adolph Coors Foundation, the Anti-Defamation League, the Columbia Charitable Foundation, Shapell Industries, Inc., the Robert I. Wishnick Foundation, the National Envelope Corporation, the American Gathering of Jewish Holocaust Survivors, Colorado Photographic Arts Center, Eastman Kodak Company, Hasselblad USA, Inc., Polaroid Corporation, ILFORD Photo, Pallas Photo of Denver, Advanced Digital Imaging, Inc., Digital World Images, the Oster Family Foundation, Dyna-Lite, Inc., Chimera, Mechano Engineering Co., and Bobe Minde Charity.

There were other friends and students who extended their hands and their hearts as this odyssey moved from vision to reality. To all of them, and to my beloved children, Joy, Dean, and Kris, I am deeply grateful for their support and encouragement. All have touched my heart.

Finally, this book, the national exhibition, and the CD-ROM never would have become a reality without the dedication, concentration, quiet resolve, and thousands of hours of effort contributed by Linda Raper, my life partner and committed associate. Her resourcefulness, skills, talents, and wise counsel have served as an ongoing source of support for me during the past five years. She has inspired the vision and has invested her soul so others could be touched by the images and moved by the messages. I shall remain eternally grateful for her service to this project.

About the Photographer & the Writer

NICK DEL CALZO

He began his journalistic career in 1967 with the *St. Louis Globe-Democrat,* where he was a reporter for five years. In 1992, after 25 years as a public relations consultant operating his own firm, he elected to pursue documentary photography as his third career. His portrait work has won numerous national awards. *The Triumphant Spirit* project, which also consists of a national exhibition and a CD-ROM, was his first major, self-directed undertaking.

RENEE ROCKFORD

She is the daughter of a Holocaust Survivor and has traveled with her father throughout the world in search of information about his family. In 1981, she covered the first World Gathering of Jewish Holocaust Survivors in Israel for two U.S. newspapers, and for more than 15 years, worked as a print and broadcast journalist. She now works independently as a media consultant.

Notes & Photographic Sites

Every reasonable effort was made to research and verify the historical accuracy of the names of the ghettos, concentration camps, places of birth, and residences of the individuals named herein, and all other site-specific references.

A partial list of the reference sources is included in the bibliography. In addition, we wish to acknowledge the research assistance of the U.S. Holocaust Memorial Museum, Martyrs Holocaust Memorial and Museum, Holocaust Museum Houston, and the Denver Public Library.

Bass, Harry: Holocaust Memorial Monument, Philadelphia, PA

Bram, David: Temple Shalom, Colorado Springs, CO

Bruk, Selene: Suva Intermediate School, Bel Gardens, CA

Chase, David T.: Jacob K. Javits Convention Center, New York, NY

Chester, Simon: Jewish Community Center, Mercer Island, WA

Clary, Robert: Simon Wiesenthal Center, Los Angeles, CA

England, Fred: East Denver Orthodox Synagogue, Denver, CO

Federman, Vera: Library of Temple De Hirsch Sinai, Seattle, WA

Firestone, Renee: The Yellow Star by Peter Sohler, Simon Wiesenthal Center, Los Angeles, CA

Fischer, Anna & Benno: Martyrs Memorial and Museum, Los Angeles, CA

Foxman, Abraham: United Nations, New York, NY

Ganor, Solly: Holocaust Oral History Project, San Francisco, CA

Goldfeier, Angie & Moritz: Statue of Liberty National Monument, New York Harbor, NY

Goldrich, Jona: Los Angeles Holocaust Monument, Pan Pacific Park, Los Angeles, CA

Harte, Roman I.: American Society of Cinematographers, Hollywood, CA

Heller, Fanya: The Jewish Museum, New York, NY

Isaacman, Clara: Logan Circle, Philadelphia, PA

Kaye, Ann & Ed: Herzl Ner Tamid Synagogue, Mercer Island, WA

Keneally, Thomas: Photo by Kerry Klayman

Kent, Roman: School playground in New York, NY

Keren, Kristine: Central Park Plaza, New York, NY

Lantos, Tom & Annette: Rayburn Office Building, Washington, DC

Loen, Masha: Martyrs Memorial and Museum, Los Angeles, CA

Luksenburg, Helen: Lincoln Memorial, Washington, DC

Margosis, Michel: U.S. Holocaust Memorial Museum, Washington, DC

Meed, Benjamin: Offices of the American Gathering of Jewish Holocaust Survivors, New York, NY

Meller, Jacob: Martyrs Memorial and Museum, Los Angeles, CA

Mermelstein, Melvin: Auschwitz Study Foundation, Huntington Beach, CA

Michel, Ernest W.: United Jewish Appeal-Federation of Jewish Philanthropies of New York, Inc., New York, NY

Millman, Edith: Holocaust Oral History Archive of Gratz College, Melrose Park, PA

Morgan, Bill: Holocaust Museum Houston, Houston, TX

Okron, Eli: Holocaust Memorial Monument, Philadelphia, PA

Page, Leopold: Los Angeles Holocaust Memorial, Pan Pacific Park, Los Angeles, CA

Pantirer, Murray: Holocaust Memorial at Liberty State Park, Jersey City, NJ

Pechman, Maurice: Los Angeles Holocaust Memorial, Pan Pacific Park, Los Angeles, CA

Resnick, Abe: The Holocaust Memorial, Miami Beach, FL

Schaffer, Irving: BMH Congregation, Denver, CO

Schwarzbart, Paul: Classroom at the University of California at Berkeley Extension, San Francisco, CA

Shapell, Nathan: School playground in Los Angeles, CA

Steiman, Morris: Liberty Bell, Philadelphia, PA

Taube, Herman: Lafayette Square, Washington, DC

Tec, Nechama: New York City Public Library, New York, NY

Thaler, Michael: "The Holocaust," a 1984 memorial sculptural installation by George Segal, Lincoln Park, San Francisco, CA

Urbach, Solomon: Liberty State Park, Jersey City, NJ

BIBLIOGRAPHY

Most of the information contained in the foregoing stories resulted from personal interviews and/or supplemental documentation provided solely by the subjects. In a few instances, the subjects referred us to previously written accounts and/or materials approved by them.

Altschuler, David A. *We Remember the Holocaust.* New York: Holt, 1989.

Berenbaum, Ph.D., Michael. *The World Must Know: The History of the Holocaust as Told in the United States Holocaust Memorial Museum.* Boston, MA: Little, Brown and Company, 1993. (Chase, Karski, Lantos)

Blatt, Thomas. *From the Ashes of Sobibor: A Story of Survival.* Evanston, IL: Northwestern University Press, 1997.

Blatt, Thomas. *Sobibor: The Forgotten Revolt.* Issaquah, WA: HEP Publishers, 1996.

Block, Gay, and Makla Drucker. *Portraits of Moral Courage in the Holocaust.* New York: Holmes and Meier, 1992.

Cargas, Harry James. *Voices from the Holocaust.* Lexington, KY: University Press of Kentucky, 1993.

Diament, Freddy E. "We Are the Last Victims." *Jewish Spectator,* April 1968.

Frank, Anne. *The Diary of a Young Girl.* New York: Globe, 1958.

Ganor, Solly. *Light One Candle: A Survivor's Tale from Lithuania to Jerusalem.* New York: Kodansha America, 1995.

Gilbert, Martin. *Atlas of the Holocaust.* New York: William Morrow, 1993.

Grobman, Alex. *Those Who Dared: Rescuers and Rescued: A Teaching Guide for Secondary Schools.* Los Angeles, CA: Martyrs Memorial and Museum of the Holocaust of The Jewish Federation, 1995.

Grobman, Alex, and Daniel Landes, eds. *Genocide: Critical Issues of the Holocaust.* Chappaqua, NY: Rossell, 1983.

Halbreich, Siegfried. *Before—During—After.* New York: Vantage Press, 1991.

Heller, Fanya Gottesfeld. *Strange and Unexpected Love.* Hoboken, NJ: KTAV Publishing House, Inc., 1993.

Helmreich, William B. *Against All Odds: Holocaust Survivors and the Successful Lives They Made in America.* New York: Simon & Schuster, 1992. (Foxman, Lantos, Meed, Michel, Ungar)

Horowitz, Ryszard, Jon Blair, Robert A. Sobieszek, and Barbara Kosinska. *Ryszard Horowitz.* New York: WAIF/M.M. Art Books, Inc., 1995.

Isaacman, Clara. *Clara's Story.* Philadelphia, PA: The Jewish Publication Society of America, 1984.

Karski, Jan. *The Story of a Secret State.* New York: Popular Library, 1965.

Keneally, Thomas. *Schindler's List.* New York: Simon & Schuster, 1982.

Kowalski, Isaac. "Songs to Remember." *Armed Jewish Resistance Anthology.* Brooklyn: Jewish Combatants Publishers House, 1986. (Henny Gurko)

Marshall, Robert. *In the Sewers of Lvov: A Heroic Story of Survival from the Holocaust.* New York: Macmillan Publishing Company, 1990.

Meed, Vladka. *On Both Sides of the Wall.* Israel: Hakibbutz Hameuchad Publishing House, 1972. (Benjamin Meed)

Meinbach, Anita Meyer, and Miriam Klein Kassenoff. *Memories of the Night: A Study of the Holocaust.* Torrance, CA: Frank Schaffer Publications, Inc., 1994.

Mermelstein, Mel. *By Bread Alone: The Story of a Survivor of the Nazi Holocaust.* Huntington Beach, CA: Auschwitz Study Foundation, Inc., 1979.

Michel, Ernest W. *Promises to Keep: One Man's Journey Against Incredible Odds!* New York: Barricade Books, Inc., 1993.

Mokotoff, Gary, and Sallyann Amdur Sack. *Where Once We Walked: A Guide to the Jewish Communities Destroyed in the Holocaust.* Teaneck, NJ: Avotaynu, Inc., 1991.

Paldiel, Mordecai. *The Path of the Righteous: Gentile Rescuers of the Jews During the Holocaust.* Hoboken, NJ: KTAV, 1993.

"Recalling the Holocaust Horrors." *Intermountain Jewish News,* September 30, 1983. (Irving Schaffer)

Shapell, Nathan. *Witness to the Truth.* New York: David McKay Company, Inc., 1974.

Sher, Dr. Aubrey J. *In the Shadow of Our Past Lest We Forget.* Los Angeles, CA: Yeshiva Gedolah of Los Angeles, 1994. (Codikow, Firestone, Goldrich, Kort, Page, Pechman)

Taube, Herman. *KYZYL Kishlak-Refugee Village.* Washington, DC: Olami Press, 1993.

Taube, Herman. *My Baltimore Landsmen.* Tel Aviv, Israel: Olami Press, 1994.

Tec, Nechama. *Defiance: The Bielski Partisans.* New York: Oxford University Press, 1993.

Tec, Nechama. *Dry Tears: The Story of a Lost Childhood.* New York: Oxford University Press, 1982.

Weissman-Klein, Gerda. *Promise of a New Spring.* Chappaqua, NY: Rossell Books, 1982.

Wiesel, Elie. *Night.* New York: Avon, 1969.

Wood, E. Thomas, and Stanislaw M. Jankowski. *Karski: How One Man Tried to Stop the Holocaust.* New York: John Wiley & Sons, Inc., 1994.

Zelon, Charlotte, and The "1939" Club. *The Indestructible Spirit: The "1939" Club.* Lomita, CA: King Printing, 1994. (Diament, Halbreich, Goetz, Bruk, Page)

Zuckerman, Abraham. *A Voice in the Chorus.* Hoboken, NJ: KTAV Publishing House, Inc., 1991.

INDEX